For Mia

Published in 2011 by Stewart, Tabori & Chang
An imprint of ABRAMS

Library of Congress Cataloging-in-Publication Data
Bernard, Wendy.
Custom knits 2 / by Wendy Bernard ; photography by Printer Hall.
p. cm.
"STC Craft/A Melanie Falick book."
ISBN 978-1-58479-938-2 (alk. paper)

1. Knitting—Patterns. 2. Sweaters. I. Title. II. Title: Custom knits two.

TT825.B3962 2011
746.43'2—dc22

2011000666

Editor: Liana Allday
Designer: Anna Christian
Production Manager: Tina Cameron

The text of this book was composed in Pastonchi and Sassoon.

Printed and bound in China
10 9 8 7 6 5 4 3 2 1

115 West 18th Street
New York, NY 10011
www.abramsbooks.com

custom knits 2

More Top-Down and Improvisational Techniques

Wendy Bernard *photographs by Printer Hall*
photostyling by Mark Auria

STC Craft | A Melanie Falick Book ✦ New York

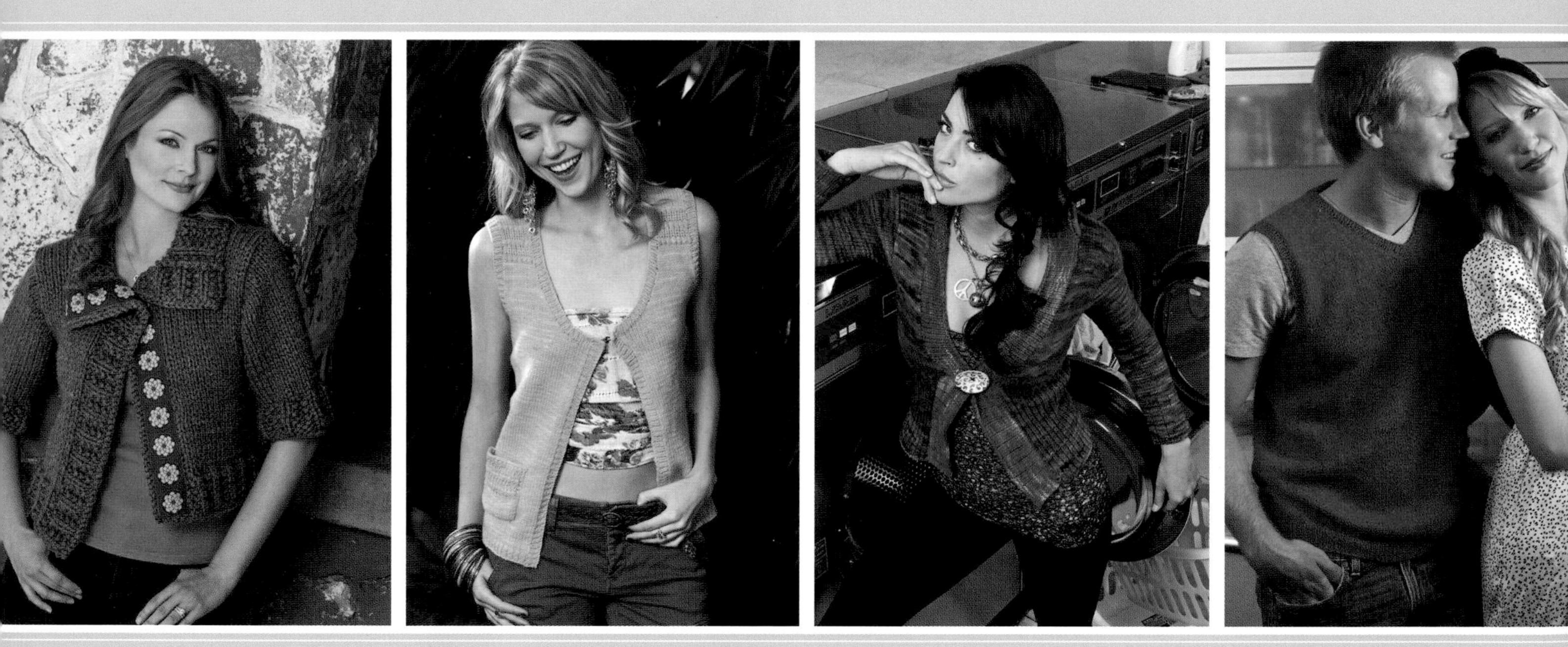

CONTENTS

INTRODUCTION

When my sweet daughter was an infant, a wise woman who had many children gave me the best advice. She told me that when it comes to raising a child and teaching her pretty much anything, I should always "begin with the end in mind." This philosophy has served me well over the years. Whether it's bedtime rituals, daily hygiene, eating right, or basically any other skill I can teach her, each time I begin with the end in mind, things inevitably work out smoothly.

The same could be said of my experience designing the patterns and writing the text for my first book, *Custom Knits.* (And they do say that writing a book can be a lot like having a baby.) I recall that if I carefully preplanned and knew exactly how I wanted a design to turn out, I was better equipped to sidestep the many minor disasters so many of us knitters face. But if I skipped some steps in the planning phase, I'd wind up having a variety of niggling doubts floating above my head as I knit: that the garment wouldn't end up looking the way I had imagined, or that the sleeves weren't shaped quite right. After a handful of starts, stops, and frogging episodes, I came to understand that if I started out with the end in mind, checking (and rechecking) my progress against my initial sketches and trying it on as I worked to make sure the measurements were right, the outcome would end up matching my initial expectations. Not only that, the process would be smooth, fast, and fun.

So it's no surprise that for my next book (which you are holding in your hands), I decided to emphasize the philosophy of starting with the end in mind and thinking while you're knitting. What do I want to make? How do I want it to look? How will I make that happen? To make a garment in the "Custom Knits" style, you have to go beyond swatching and make a true plan of attack; then you need to check your progress many times from beginning to end. *Custom Knits* was all about personalizing a top-down pattern by changing sleeves, necklines, and other sweater elements to your liking. In *Custom Knits 2,* I've picked up where the first book left off by giving you a host of new techniques, formulas, tips, and tricks to employ while knitting from the top down, plus a whole new suite of patterns and variations—this time for the whole family—on which to try out what you've learned.

In keeping with the spirit of "beginning with the end in mind," I've organized this book by technique, starting each chapter with a tutorial and then following it up with patterns that show how the technique can be put into practice. I've split these new and varied techniques into five chapters: Basic Training, He Said She Said, Tailored Raglans, Knitting Swaps, and Starting from Scratch. I begin by showing you how to preplan your sweater so that you'll know exactly how to customize the pattern. In the next chapter, Basic Training, I cover easy ways to tailor the fit of an existing pattern and how to add appendages like hoods or sleeves. The third chapter, He Said, She Said, teaches you how to upsize or downsize a sweater to fit anyone of any age or gender, and how to feminize or masculinize the pattern, as needed. In the fourth chapter, I show you how to customize a raglan sweater—the trickiest of all sweater types if you want to get a good fit. In the fifth chapter, I show you how to substitute different yarns at different gauges and swap out stitch patterns or motifs. The final chapter includes formulas for knitting two different sweater styles from scratch, using any yarn you like.

As with my first book, all of the 25 new top-down knitting patterns can be made just as they're written or customized as you please. The variations and "Make It Your Own" boxes throughout are meant to give you some good ideas for alterations and to get your creative juices flowing.

Whatever you do (and no matter who you're knitting for), try to begin with the end in mind. For me, that *usually* means knitting from the top down, and it always means doing careful preplanning. Most important, it is my hope that as you apply the techniques in this book to the garments you are creating, you will have the confidence to use patterns more as a guide than a hard-and-fast rule book that must be followed. When you knit with confidence and think while you work, you can personalize every detail and decide exactly how and when you want to veer from the pattern. Then, when you bind off that last stitch, you'll be proud to see that it turned out just the way you wanted.

Wendy.

CHAPTER 1

Preplanning the Perfect Sweater: Begin with the End in Mind

Before you start knitting the patterns in this book, examine the entire pattern, including the directions and the schematic, and compare the wearer's measurements to the finished pattern. Think about the wearer's likes and dislikes and figure out if you can customize the pattern so that it will perfectly suit her or his style and body type. And don't forget to try on as you go!

All of us at one time or another suffer from the affliction I call Knitting Pattern Dysmorphic Syndrome (KPDS). You know what I'm talking about: It's that sweeping emotional kick in the head that happens to you when you spot a pattern that you absolutely must knit for yourself or someone else ASAP. The problem with KPDS is that you are less likely to think about things like shaping, sleeve length, armhole depth, upper arm circumference . . . you know, the stuff that truly makes the garment a success.

When you are under the spell of KPDS, it isn't that you can't or shouldn't make the garment. It just means that you need to take a moment and envision yourself or the person for whom you are knitting and realistically lay out, in your mind or on paper, any changes that you might need to make to the fit or the design. Before you get started, here is a list of things you'll want to do:

✦ Take the wearer's measurements.

✦ Compare the measurements to the schematic (or fill out the "How Do I Veer from the Norm?" form at right).

✦ Decide on the amount of ease you want.

✦ Jot down notes about areas in the pattern that need to be altered, and, if necessary, create your own schematic with your own measurements, noting where they differ from the pattern.

✦ Preplan sections of the pattern where you need to add or subtract shaping (see page 18).

✦ If you want to add, remove, or alter sweater elements, find information in *Custom Knits* and in this book to help you do so.

✦ If you're converting the pattern for a person of a different age or gender, determine which features need to be altered (see page 48).

✦ Calculate how much yarn you will need if you are adding sleeves or a hood, width, circumference, or length (see page 15).

What's My Shape?

When knitwear designers make patterns, it's common for them to adhere to a set of "sizing standards." These charts are created by taking average measurements from a sample of many people. Does this mean that if you have a 40″ chest that the corresponding waist size on the "standard" chart will also be your size? Probably not. That is why it is helpful to see how your own shape veers from the "norm" when it comes to knit patterns. To do this, fill out the form at right with your own measurements and then fill in the finished measurements from the pattern in the column next to it. Then, fill in the amount of ease you want to add to or subtract from a section or the amount of length you'd like to add or take away from the sleeves or body. Then tally the columns to figure out what your new measurements will be. It may be helpful at this stage to draw a new schematic showing your customized measurements so you have a blueprint of how it will all fit together. You may also want to highlight areas in your new schematic as a reminder that you need to make an adjustment when you reach that point in the pattern.

So What Is *Ease* Anyway?

Simply put, ease is the way a garment fits your body. A sweater with "positive ease" fits loosely in the body, arms, or hips, and a sweater with "negative ease" is tighter fitting. Ease is totally personal. If you like a super-loose garment, go for more than a few inches. Seriously, there are patterns out there that call for up to 6″ of positive ease or more! Then there are patterns where it is customary to have at least three inches of negative ease so that it stretches across the body. To find out what type of ease you're most likely to wear, lay a favorite sweater on a flat surface. Take measurements across the garment at the chest, waist, hip, and upper arm. Then measure your own body and compare it to these measurements. You may discover that you prefer positive ease in one area but not in another, or vice versa. The key is to explore and discover your preferences.

How Do I Veer from the Norm?

Fill out the measurements on this worksheet to make a custom-fitted garment.

	PATTERN	YOU	ADD/SUBTRACT EASE	NEW MEASUREMENTS
Crossback: *measure from shoulder bump to shoulder bump*	______	______	______	______
Shoulder: *measure from neck to end of shoulder*	______	______	______	______
Underarm depth: *measure depth of favorite sweater or from top center shoulder to underarm*	______	______	______	______
Chest: *measure around chest at fullest part*	______	______	______	______
Waist: *measure around waist*	______	______	______	______
Hip: *measure around fullest part of hip*	______	______	______	______
Length: *measure from top of shoulder to where you want hem to land*	______	______	______	______
Upper arm circumference: *measure around upper arm*	______	______	______	______
Sleeve length: *measure from underarm to where you want sleeve to end*	______	______	______	______

Trying on as You Go

One of the benefits of knitting from the top and in one piece is that you have the option of trying on the garment as you work your way through the pattern. When you knit patterns flat and in pieces, it's possible to hold a pattern piece up to your body to check length, but you can't really visualize how the garment will end up fitting once it's sewn together. When you try on an in-progress top-down garment, however, you'll be able to make adjustments as you go. Whether you're trying the garment on yourself, putting it on a dress form, or throwing it over someone else's head, it's important to understand a thing or two about this key step. For instance, how do you go about "trying on as you go"? Won't your stitches fall off the needles when you pull it over your head? At what key points should you try it on? Here are some pointers.

SECURING YOUR STITCHES

When working patterns in the round from the top down, we typically work the body using 29"-long or longer circular needles. If you're new to top-down knitting, you may have a confused moment when you try on your garment and realize that your circular needle will never fit over your shoulders (let alone your bust) without stitches flying off the needles and unraveling. So let me clear things up: In order to try on the garment as you go, you need to put your stitches on a holder. There are several ways to do this, and it's up to you to decide which method to use.

One simple method is to thread a tapestry needle with a length of slippery waste yarn at least twice the circumference of the sweater and run it through each live stitch, pulling the stitches off the needle as you go. When you're done trying on, you'll need to load all of those stitches back onto your needle, remove the waste yarn, and continue knitting.

If you happen to have another long circular needle in the same size, here's another way to secure your stitches when you go to try on: work half of the stitches from the body onto the second needle, then try on the garment with the two circular needles holding the live stitches. In some cases you might need a third circular needle to accommodate a larger circumference.

If you don't happen to have a needle the same size as your working needle, you can *slip* the stitches onto a second needle instead of knitting them, so your gauge on that row won't be disturbed. If you do this, make sure that the second needle size is smaller, not larger—otherwise you might distort your stitches.

Some knitters don't particularly enjoy putting their stitches on holders in order to try on the garment, but in all honesty, it takes just a few minutes and it's totally worth it. Imagine, for instance, if you didn't try on your sweater before you joined the front and back under the arms, and discovered much later that your armhole is too long? It would take hours to rip out the mistake and re-knit the sweater compared to just five or ten minutes to put your stitches on holders.

KEY POINTS FOR TRYING ON

When working any type of top-down sweater, there are a few key points when you'll need to try it on. Of course, you can try it as much as you like, but these are the points when I usually pause and put the garment on myself, my dress form, or the person for whom I'm knitting.

✦ Before the two sides of the neckline are joined, to test the shape and depth of the neckline.

✦ Before joining under the arms, to double-check the depth of the armholes.

✦ Before waist shaping occurs, to be sure that the first set of decreases are placed perfectly.

✦ Before beginning a hem or ribbing at the bottom of the garment, to test the garment's length.

✦ When the sleeves reach the upper arm, try on to test the circumference, then try on again when nearly finished to test the length. You may not need to place the stitches on waste yarn—your circular needle will likely hold all the stitches.

Easy Ways to Calculate How Much Yarn You Need

Whether you're converting gauge, upsizing or downsizing a sweater, or adding an element like a hood or sleeves, you'll need to make sure you're buying the correct amount of yarn. Running out of yarn is never fun, and having a ton left over that you can't return to the store isn't either. Here are a couple of ways to figure out how much yarn you'll need.

1 Refer to a yarn requirement chart, such as Ann Budd's *The Knitter's Handy Guide to Yarn Requirements* (Interweave Press). This is particularly helpful if you're converting gauge, since the yarn requirement charts cover multiple gauges. You should be able to compare the original starting gauge requirements to the one you're changing to, and then reverse your calculations and back into the required yardage by making a simple mathematical equation or two. For example, say your chosen vest pattern has a gauge of 6 stitches to the inch and requires 600 yards for your size. Looking at your yarn requirement chart, you'll find that a generic vest at that gauge requires 749 yards. Looking at these numbers in a statistical sense, you could surmise that your chosen pattern requires approximately 80 percent of what the yarn requirement charts say (600 yards for your pattern / 749 yards for the generic pattern = .80, or 80 percent).

To fine-tune your estimate, you could look at the requirements for a generic vest at your "new" gauge, which we'll say is 5 stitches to the inch. The chart says that, at that gauge, a generic vest would require 529 yards at that same size. So, using simple math you could guess that the pattern you want to knit would probably only require 80 percent of what a generic vest would require, 529 yards x 80% = 423.2, or about 423 yards. To be safe, you might want to check the return policy at your yarn shop or online store and purchase one extra ball "just in case."

2 Calculate your yarn requirements based on the pattern's schematic. Let's say that you want to add long sleeves to a short-sleeve cardigan with a gauge of 5 rows per inch. First look at the schematic and make note of the length of the current sleeve, then note the length of the section you are adding. Next determine the width of the sleeve both at the cuff and the top of the section that you are adding. Picture each sleeve laid out flat. The basic shape of each sleeve (assuming the cuff is narrower than the top of the sleeve) is a trapezoid. If you turn one sleeve 180 degrees, and place it next to the other, you see that together they form a parallelogram (see illustration below). To get the width of the parallelogram, simply add the width of the cuff and the width of the top of the section that you are adding. For example, if your cuff measurement is 9" and the top of the section that you are adding is 18", then the width will measure 27". Multiply the length of the section you are adding by 5 rows per inch. This will give you the total number of rows for the rectangle (15" × 5 rows per inch = 75 rows). Since one row of Stockinette stitch takes a length of yarn approximately three times the width of the piece you are knitting, if you take the parallelogram as if it were one whole piece, each row that is 27" wide will take 81" of yarn (27" × 3). So multiply 81" of yarn times 75 rows for the parallelogram, and you'll get 6,075" of yarn. Divide that by 36" to find out the yardage, and you'll arrive at 168.75 yards for both sleeves. Calculate an additional 10 percent or so for "padding" (185.6 yards). This method for calculating yarn will also work for adding length to a sweater or adding a collar (such as a turtleneck) that isn't called for in the pattern. If there is no shaping, you will already be working with a simple rectangle, which should make your calculations easier. If you have shaping, you may be able to divide sections into trapezoids as above. If you're uncomfortable with using this formula, use a basic rectangle instead, but know that you will likely have a lot of yarn left over—not such a bad thing!

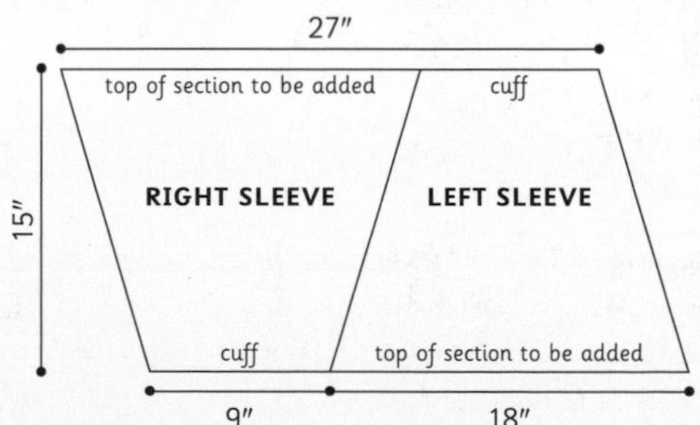

Note: Sleeves will be worked in the round, but are pictured here as if they are worked flat, for the purpose of illustrating the calculations. The Left Sleeve is pictured after turning it 180°.

1. Pour detergent* & fabric
softener into dispenser on top
of machine.
Double Load
Triple Load
Maxi Load
2. Load clothes and latch door.
3. Select wash cycle.
4. Insert coins to start washer.
5. Add bleach when bleach
light comes on.
TRIPLE
THOROUGHBRED
400
DEXTER
WARNING

CHAPTER 2

Basic Training: Simple Alterations and Add-Ons

Sometimes the sweater pattern you want to make is just about right but needs a few minor adjustments. In this chapter, you'll find a variety of ways to tweak an existing pattern so that it will fit and look just right—whether you want to make the fit snugger or roomier or add an extra design feature like a hood or sleeves.

SIMPLE ELEMENTS TO TWEAK

You can make these basic alterations to almost any top-down sweater style.

Basic Alteration 1: Shaping with Short Rows

The trick to tailoring just about any garment is to add short rows at key spots. This works for almost all garment types, including cardigans, pullovers, and vests.

Short rows are partial rows of knitting wherein you work back and forth over a particular area, inconspicuously adding extra fabric where it's needed. Short rows can be used to create all sorts of things, from capped sleeves to sock heels, but they are often used in the bust section of a garment to accommodate those with ample chests, and in the upper back section to raise the neck in round yoke sweaters (which have a tendency to fall lower than desired at the back neck). You can even use short rows to accommodate a round belly or a Dowager's hump. (For a tutorial on how to work short rows, see page 156.)

A lot of knitters don't realize that short rows are an option, and they wind up making a sweater that is (insert dramatic music here) a size too big! Knitting a larger size when you really only need, say, another inch or two of ease in just one area is a tragedy because not only are you sizing up that one measurement, you're also committing to a wider back measurement, deeper armholes, longer sleeves, and in many cases, a longer body, too. By short row shaping in your target areas, you can custom-fit your garment without casting on more stitches or significantly changing the look.

ADDING SHORT ROWS TO THE BUST

If you happen to be someone whose chest-to-waist-to-hip ratio differs from the norm—and let me tell you, I think most of ours do—you might benefit from short rows in the bust area. But which size sweater do you choose to make? If your chest is larger than what is called for, but the rest of the pattern will fit, pick the size that has a crossback measurement closest to yours and do a few short rows in the chest area when you get to that point in your knitting. Then pick the philosophy that works best for you.

Philosophy 1

If you have a B cup and want some extra fabric at the bust in an otherwise close-fitting sweater, work a couple sets of short rows on either side of the front, which, depending on your row gauge, will give you an extra inch or two of space. And then for each cup size above a B, on each following short row, work approximately one inch of stitches before wrapping the next stitch. This isn't scientific, and your mileage will vary, but it's one way you could go about it. Here's how the formula breaks down, by cup size:

For a B Cup:

Row 1: On the front, just above the fullest part of your chest, work to within 1″ of the left underarm, wrap the next stitch, and turn.

Row 2: Working on the wrong side, work to the opposite side, to within an inch of the right underarm, wrap the next stitch, and turn.

Row 3: Work across to a little less than 1″ before the previous wrap, wrap the next stitch, and turn. (For example: If your stitch gauge is 5 stitches to the inch, work 4 stitches, wrap the next stitch, and turn.)

Row 4: Working on the wrong side, repeat Row 3.

For a C Cup:

Work Rows 1–4 as for B cup, then repeat Rows 3 and 4 one extra time, equaling a total of three sets of short rows (3 short rows on each side, 6 rows in all).

For a D Cup:

Work Rows 1–4 as for B cup, then repeat Rows 3 and 4 TWO extra times, equaling a total of four sets of short rows.

For Larger Bust Sizes:

Add one extra pair of short rows for each cup size above a D cup, working your way from near the underarm toward the center of the sweater, and spacing wraps on short rows closer than an inch together, if necessary, so that the short rows stay off to the side of your bust.

Philosophy 2

The second philosophy is more exact, telling you precisely where and how to place short rows based on your measurements. It takes a little more time, but will give you a truly custom fit.

Determine Number of Short Rows

To determine the number of short rows you need, refer to your original gauge swatch (or a section of the sweater if you've already started) and jot down your stitch and row gauge. For the sake of having an example, say that you have a stitch gauge of 5 and a row gauge of 6. The next step is to take two measurements: the length from your back neck down to where you want the sweater to end, and the length of the front from the top of the shoulder down to the same point. Then, subtract the back length from the front. As an example, say the back measurement is 22" and the front measurement is 24". So, 24" (front) – 22" (back) = 2" of short rows. Then, multiply the number of inches by your row gauge: 2" (short rows) x 6 (row gauge) = 12 short rows for the front. Then, divide the number of required short rows by 2 to determine how many short rows are needed on each side of the front: 12 (short rows) ÷ 2 = 6 (short rows each side).

Determine Placement of Short Rows

You can determine the placement of the short rows one of two ways. The first way is the simplest: If you're only adding a few short rows, you can try on the sweater as you go and work the required number of short rows when the length of your sweater is just above the fullest part of your bust. To do this, work the sweater to within an inch of the desired beginning point for the short rows, then on one front side, wrap and turn, work to the same place on the opposite side of the front, wrap and turn, and repeat the process, spacing the wraps and turns a few stitches from each other until you've added the required number of short rows. If you are working a cardigan, or a pullover where the front neck sides have not been joined yet, work all the short rows on one front, then repeat the process for the other front. Voilà! You're done. (For a written example of working short rows when the fronts have not been joined, see the Women's version of the Holden Jacket on page 54.)

If you require a larger number of short rows, you may need to do a few more calculations so that the last set of short rows are well placed and do not encroach on the very center front of the sweater. It's important to keep the short rows off to the sides a bit so that the wrapped stitches won't be visible right smack in the middle of your chest. Also, if your short rows begin near the underarm but wind up in the center of your chest, you might end up with a cone-shaped center front. This would not be attractive!

Short rows look best (and the sweater will fit best) if the final wrapped stitch hits the center of each breast. With that goal in mind, examine your swatch or partial section of knitting. Is it stretchy? (If it is stretchy, then the short rows will appear farther apart when the garment is worn.) Are the stitches small, close and tight? Or are they large? What about the fit of the garment? Do you expect it to be tight fitting or do you want it to flow over your body with lots of ease? You want your short row wraps to land between your armpit and the center third of your front, so it's helpful to know how you want your garment to fit and look before you calculate the placement of short rows.

To get started, take a look at the illustration at right and measure the width between the center of each breast. Alternatively, if you want your short rows to end closer to the armpits and not be so visible (certain types of yarn show the hidden wraps more than others), then widen the measurement by an inch or two.

Next, determine how many inches of width on each side are available for your short rows. To do this, take the center measurement you just calculated (8″), and subtract it from the total number of inches across your front. If your sweater is 40″ around, then the front will be half of that (20″). So, 20″ for front – 8″ (center width between ends of darts) = 12″ available for your short rows. Divide this number by 2 (two sides): 12″ available ÷ 2 = 6″ available on each side. Then multiply this number by your stitch gauge: 6″ available x 5 stitches to the inch = 30 stitches available on each side for each set of short rows.

Once you have determined how many "wraps and turns" are needed on each side of the sweater and how many stitches are available for working short rows on each side of the bust, all you have to do is divide the available stitches by the number of wraps and turns. For example, if you need 6 wraps and turns on each side of the sweater and know you have 30 stitches available on each side of the bust, divide 30 (stitches available) by 6 (wraps and turns), which comes out to 5 stitches between each wrap and turn on each side. Round the number of wraps to the nearest whole number if your division returns a fraction.

Once you've worked out this math, applying it to a sweater is easy!

IF YOU ARE WORKING A TOP-DOWN PULLOVER IN THE ROUND:

✦ Work to the location where you want your short rows to begin (top of bust).

✦ Work to 1 stitch before the end of the front, or to where you want your first short row to start (closest to the armpit). Wrap the next stitch and turn.

✦ Purl to 1 stitch before the wrong-side end of the front, wrap the next stitch and turn.

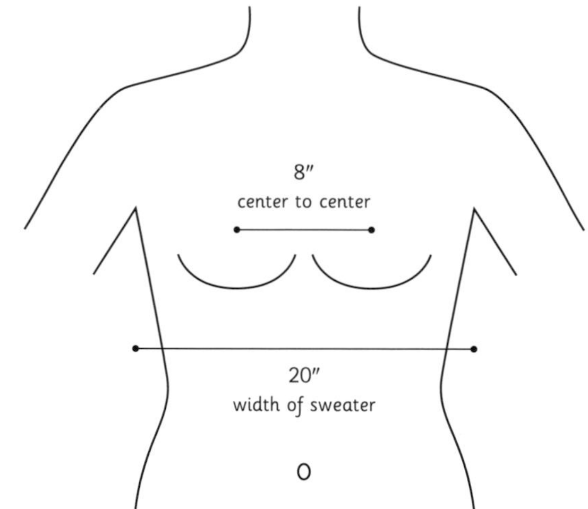

✦ Continue doing this at the interval of stitches that you determined (in this example, every fifth stitch), until you have completed the number of wraps and turns needed for each side. Remember, you will be moving in from the underarms toward the center of the front.

✦ On the next right-side row, continue working in rounds and continue to hide the wraps as you encounter them.

IF YOU ARE WORKING A TOP-DOWN CARDIGAN IN ONE PIECE:

✦ Work to the location where you want your short rows to begin (top of bust).

✦ On the next right-side row, work across the first front, across the back and to the side marker. Slip that marker, wrap the next stitch of the front, and turn.

✦ With wrong side facing, work across the back to the side marker and slip it. Wrap the next stitch and turn.

✦ Continue doing this at the interval of stitches that you determined (in this example, every fifth stitch), until you have completed the number of wraps and turns needed for each front. Remember, you will be moving in from the underarms toward the center of the fronts.

✦ Once all the short rows are complete, continue working in rows and hiding the wraps as you encounter them.

Basic Alteration 2: Adding Waist Shaping

Everyone's shape is unique, so it's up to you to determine where the waist in your sweater should land if you want a custom fit. Here are some guidelines for taking control of this all-important alteration.

With top-down patterns, waist shaping begins a certain number of inches above the back waist. (The back waist measurement is the number of inches from the back of the neck to the natural waist). Depending on the number of inches' difference between your chest measurement and your waist measurement (whether it be fewer inches or more inches for those with an ample waistline), subtract the waist measurement from the chest measurement. If you get a positive number, then you will make decreases for waist shaping. If you get a negative number, you can either knit straight, without shaping, or choose to add stitches.

Determine the number of stitches you need to subtract or add, and then determine the number of shaping increments you need to perform, plus the placement of the first set of shaping increments. For example, say you have a 40″ bust and a 34″ waist. 40″ – 34″ = 6″ to reduce. If your gauge is 6 stitches to the inch, that means you will need to reduce a total of 36 stitches (6 stitches x 6″ = 36 stitches to reduce). Since you reduce 4 stitches each decrease round (2 decreases for back and 2 for front), that means you will need a total of 9 shaping increments (36 stitches ÷ 4 decreases per round = 9 decrease rounds).

To determine where to begin the shaping, take your back waist measurement (from the base of your neck to your waist). You probably won't want to start decreasing until at least the bottom of the chest. Determine where to begin your waist shaping by looking in the mirror and measuring where you want to start and where you want to end. Assuming you want to end at your back waist, measure UP from your natural waist to where you want your decreases to begin. If you decide you have 5″ in which to make your decreases and your row count is 8 rows per inch, then you'll have 40 rounds (8 rows x 6″ = 48 rounds) to work your decreases. Now that you know that, divide your rounds by the number of increments to find out how often you'll work your decrease/increase rounds: 48 rounds ÷ 9 shaping increments = 5.3 rounds.

The most straightforward way to accomplish your shaping, then, is to work a shaping round on every fifth round, 9 times, then measure the garment. Work until the garment measures the same as your own back waist plus one inch, and then perform the same number of shaping increments for your hips (that is, if your hip measurement is the same as your chest). If it isn't, then of course, add or subtract whatever number of shaping increments you'll need for the best fit.

KNOTTED (PAGE 37) WITHOUT SLEEVES OR HOOD

KNOTTED (PAGE 41) WITH SLEEVES AND HOOD

Basic Alteration 3: Add-Ons

I can't tell you how many times I've heard from knitters that they want to knit a sweater or cardigan with a hood, but can't find a hoodie pattern that they like. Or that they'd love to add sleeves to a tank top pattern but they're not sure how to do it. Sometimes, too, knitters want the look and structure of seams in their garment, but they'd much prefer to knit it in the round. Well, guess what? All of these things can be added to existing patterns. Here's how.

ADDING A HOOD TO A CARDIGAN OR PULLOVER

There are a handful of methods for adding hoods, and most are worked by picking up stitches around the neckline and then working without shaping to the desired length. A Three-Needle Bind-Off is typically used to close the top of the hood. The problem with this construction is twofold: 1) the hood ends up with an ugly seam running along the top, and 2) it creates a nifty pointed effect that's pretty dang cute on a toddler, but on a grown adult? No thank you, at least not for me. To avoid the effect of the elfin hood, I like to use some shaping to give the top of the hood a more natural and rounded look. I also use Kitchener stitch to close the top seam invisibly. If you prefer not to use Kitchener stitch and don't mind a seam at the top of the hood, feel free to use Three-Needle Bind-Off to join the halves, or bind off the stitches and sew the top halves together. This technique works best for a cardigan or a pullover with a V-neck or relatively deep scoop neck.

1 If there are reserved back neck stitches, prepare for your hood by placing them on a spare needle or the left-hand end of a circular needle. If there are no reserved back neck stitches, you'll need to pick up and knit stitches from shoulder to shoulder during the next step.

2 Beginning at a row about 2″ below the right front shoulder, pick up and knit stitches all the way around to the center of the back neck, place a marker, and then continue to the other side, ending approximately 2″ below the left front shoulder. Turn.

3 Beginning with a wrong-side row, work flat in desired stitch pattern for 10–11", depending on what size hood you would like. The shaping at the top of the hood typically takes about 3" to complete, so be sure that you work to 3" before where you want the hood to end. *Note: In this book, the hoods are on the shorter side because they're considered more ornamental. For one that is longer, work it a little past the given length, then try it on to see if it is long enough for you.*

4 When you have reached your desired length (less 3"), ending with a wrong-side row, finish off the hood as follows: Increase 1 stitch at each neck edge and decrease 2 stitches at center back this row, then every other row 8 times, as follows: K1, m1, knit to 3 sts before center marker, ssk, k1, sm, k1, k2tog, work to last st, m1, k1. Work even for 1 row.

5 Fold hood in half and graft halves together using Kitchener stitch (see Special Techniques, page 152). If you prefer, you may bind off all sts and sew the halves together, or use Three-Needle BO (see Special Techniques, page 153) to bind off the stitches. Follow the remainder of the pattern by adding edgings, but include the front edge of the hood when finishing.

AFTERTHOUGHT SLEEVES

If you're making a top-down set-in-sleeve garment, you can add afterthought sleeves by picking up from the armholes and working in the round down to the cuff. With afterthought sleeves, you will have the opportunity to try on as you go and change the shape and length. Note that if you add sleeves where there weren't any, you may need more yarn (see Easy Ways to Calculate How Much Yarn You Need, page 15).

Formula for Afterthought Sleeves

To work a seamless set-in sleeve, you'll need a circular needle or two for working in the round. If the armhole is large enough, use a 16"-long circular needle and work in the round. If the armhole is smaller, use two circulars at once or work in the round using double-pointed needles. You will also need 6 markers in 3 colors. *Note: There might be times when you want to subtract sleeves instead of add them. To make a set-in sleeve sweater sleeveless, just work the pattern as written, and then pick up stitches around the armhole as directed in the pattern (or follow the steps here). Work about an inch of ribbing or a nonrolling stitch pattern in the round, and bind off.*

1 Pick up and knit stitches evenly around the armhole, approximately 2 stitches for every 3 rows, marking the exact top of the shoulder with a marker as you go. Also place a marker in the same color at the bottom center of the armhole for the beginning of the round (do not use this color marker for any other purpose). You should have the same number of stitches on either side between the top of shoulder marker and the beginning of round marker (see illustration on page 24).

2 Divide the number of stitches you picked up by 3 (rounding up or down to a number divisible by 2). This is the number of stitches you will have at the top of your sleeve cap, with half of these stitches on each side of the top of shoulder marker.

3 Note where on the back and front you began increasing stitches for your underarm shaping. (Refer to the pattern or look at the shaping of your armhole to identify those stitches. They will be single-stitch increases (m1's and cast-on stitches placed at the bottom of the underarm.)

4 Knit your way around the armhole (or begin the stitch pattern if there is one), and place a marker of a second color (call this marker A; see illustration on page 24) at the point where you *started* (if you worked the armhole from the top down) or *finished* (if you worked from the bottom up), adding underarm stitches either by increasing or casting on. Then, knowing how many stitches make up a third of the total sleeve stitches, as you work, place 1 marker of a third color (call these markers B) before and after these stitches, remembering that half of the stitches should be on either side of the top of shoulder marker. Continue working around the armhole and place a marker of the second color (A) where you *started* (or *finished*) your underarm increases. *Note: You may, if you prefer, place removable markers in the appropriate places before you begin the second round. Or, after you have done this a few times, you may decide to omit the first knitted round and just place your markers as you initially pick up your stitches. This will produce an even smoother result. If, however, you are working a stitch pattern on the sleeves, it may help to work 1 round in the pattern before beginning the cap shaping.*

5 Take a look at your markers: You will see that you have a beginning of the round marker, 2 markers of the same color (A) on either side of the underarm stitches and 2 markers of the same color (B) marking the top third stitches, with a top of shoulder marker centered between them. (See illustration below.)

6 Now it is time to begin your short rows (see Special Techniques, page 156), which will shape the top of the sleeve. Having marked your armhole, work around the armhole, slipping the first 3 markers, all the way past the top of the sleeve to the farthest marker separating the top third of the sleeve from the rest of the stitches (B). Slip this marker and wrap the next stitch. Turn the work, and work across the wrong-side row across the center third of the sleeve (which has the top of shoulder marker in the middle of it) to the marker on the opposite side of the center third stitches (B), slip the marker and wrap the next stitch. Turn the work again, and work across the right-side row across the center third to 1 stitch beyond the place where you stopped before. Wrap the next stitch and turn. Again, work across the wrong-side row across the center third to 1 stitch beyond the previous stopping place, wrap the next stitch, and turn the work. Continue in this manner, working short rows back and forth across the sleeve cap and taking 1 more stitch from each side before you make a turn. Hide each wrapped stitch as you come to it.

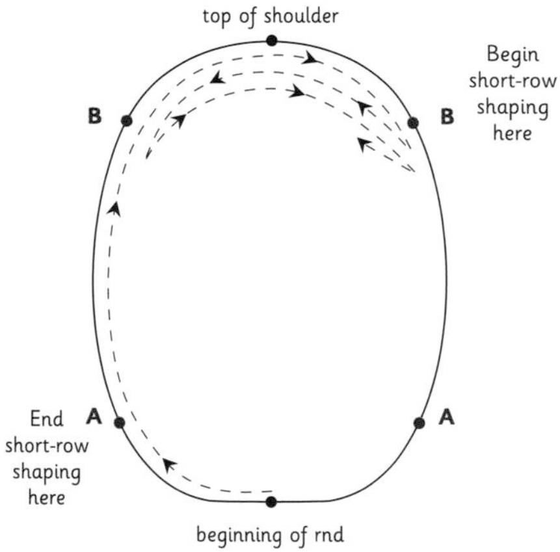

7 When you have worked your way to the markers separating the underarm stitches from the others on both sides (A), you have completed the sleeve cap. Work a final right-side row across the remaining underarm stitches, hiding the leftover wrap as you come to it. Note that depending on how many stitches you cast on, and how you divided them up, you may find you have an extra stitch between your last wrapped stitch and the A marker. You may either work one more set of short rows, going just past the markers, or you may consider your short row shaping complete, and continue on.

8 Work your sleeve in the round, as desired, adding shaping as you go.

ADDING SEAMS AND STRUCTURE TO IN-THE-ROUND SWEATERS

The benefits of working top down and in the round are many, but most people enjoy this approach because they can avoid sewing the pieces together at the end. There are times, however, when adding structure to an otherwise seamless garment is a good idea. For instance in a seamless garment, it can be challenging to find the folds at the sides when blocking. Other times, knitters feel that their seamless sweater "doesn't hang right" or lacks structure. The following tips will help if you decide your garment needs extra structure or durability.

Phoney Seams

"Phoney seams," which Elizabeth Zimmermann talks about in her book *Knitting Workshop*, are simple but very effective. Simply drop stitches along the sides of the body and allow them to unravel, then pick them up again with a crochet hook and hook up toward the top. She suggests hooking up 2 runner stitches (a runner is that ladder between stitches that you pick up when you work a make one) to every 3 rounds. In other words, put the crochet hook in the first stitch at the bottom of the dropped stitch that you made, and hook the next 2 ladder threads through it. Then, hook the ladder above only. Continue up toward the top, alternating 2, then 1, then 2, then 1.

If you plan on including phoney seams, you need to plan ahead. This means that when you begin working the body of the sweater in the round down toward the hem, you will need to add 1 stitch to each underarm and mark the added stitches, so you know which stitches you will be dropping after the body is complete.

Another method for adding "seams" to the body, especially one that is mostly Stockinette stitch, is to plan ahead by adding 1 stitch for each underarm and then, instead of dropping them and hooking them up later (like Zimmermann instructs), you can place a marker as a reminder and then alternate knitting and purling those stitches to create the "look" of a seam. This method works well with sleeves, too. Just add that extra stitch and work it as for the body. Any shaping will occur on either side of this "seam" stitch.

Reinforcing Shoulders

Here are a few tips for reinforcing the shoulders, which can be especially helpful if you are knitting a larger size sweater, are working with a heavy yarn, or if there will be a good deal of length and you don't want the sweater to droop.

Bias Tape: Simply cut bias tape the width of the shoulders, and using a needle and thread, tack the length of it onto the underside where seams would otherwise go. This technique will limit the amount of stretch that can occur at the shoulder tops.

Pick Up and Knit: If you want even more support at the top of the shoulder, consider skipping the Provisional CO at the beginning of a top-down set-in sleeve pattern. Just use the cast-on of your choice, and instead of unraveling the provisional cast-on when working the front(s), simply pick up and knit the required number of stitches from the back shoulder for the right front. For the left front, carefully count the number of stitches, beginning at the outside left shoulder edge and counting toward the center neck, and begin picking up and knitting stitches from that point to the shoulder edge. The "pick-up" line acts just like a seam and will probably be more attractive than a sewn seam. Not to mention, you will have added a little extra structure where structure was needed.

Add a Line of Crochet: You can add a line of crochet stitches across the shoulder to stabilize stitches without disrupting the smooth line of a seamless area of knitting. To do this, get a crochet hook approximately the same size as the knitting needles used and the same color yarn. Make a slipknot and place it on the hook. With the wrong side of the shoulder facing (where the seam would normally be), begin at one edge, insert the hook under a purl bump, yarn over, then pull the yarnover through the loop on the hook. Continue across and fasten off. What you'll have is a stable, but still seamless, shoulder.

Double Load
Triple Load
2. Load clothes and latch door.
3. Select wash cycle.
4. Insert coins to start washer.
5. Add bleach when bleach light comes on.
Bleach Light
6. Door will remain locked and
THOROUGHBRED
400

FAVORITE HOODIE

Worked as a top-down set-in-sleeve cardigan, this close-fitting hoodie is designed to look just like a store-bought favorite I have worn over and over and over. If I could have purchased another one just like it in a different color, I would have, but this was one of those "sleeper" sweaters that I didn't realize I'd wear so often until it was no longer available in the stores. Now that I've written a similar pattern, I can whip up another one whenever I please.

PATTERN FEATURES
Top-down set-in sleeve construction, provisional cast-on, simple shaping, ribbing, picking up and knitting.

SIZES

X-Small (Small, Medium, Large, 1X-Large, 2X-Large, 3X-Large)

FINISHED MEASUREMENTS

30 (34½, 38, 42½, 46, 50½, 54)" chest, buttoned

Note: You may adjust the placement of the hook and eye and button to adjust the fit of the Hoodie.

YARN

Malabrigo Merino Worsted (100% merino wool; 216 yards / 100 grams): 5 (5, 6, 6, 7, 8, 8) #160 Verde Esperanza

NEEDLES

One 32" (80 cm) long or longer circular (circ) needle size US 7 (4.5 mm)

One or two 24" (60 cm) long or longer circular needles or one set of five double-pointed needles (dpn) size US 7 (4.5 mm), as preferred, for Sleeves

Change needle size if necessary to obtain correct gauge.

NOTIONS

Waste yarn; removable stitch marker; stitch markers in 3 colors; 1 large hook and eye; one 2" button; 6" length of ¼" wide ribbon

GAUGE

18 sts and 22 rows = 4" (10 cm) in Stockinette stitch (St st)

20 sts and 24 rows = 4" (10 cm) in 1x1 Rib

STITCH PATTERNS

1x1 Rib

(multiple of 2 sts + 1; 1-row repeat)
Row 1: *K1, p1; repeat from * to last st, k1.
Row 2: Knit the knit sts and purl the purl sts as they face you.
Repeat Row 2 for 1x1 Rib.

3x1 Rib (worked in the rnd)

(multiple of 4 sts; 1-row repeat)
All Rnds: *K3, p1; repeat from * to end.

3x1 Rib (worked flat)

(multiple of 4 sts + 3; 1-row repeat)
Row 1 (WS): *P3, k1; repeat from * to last 3 sts, p3.
Row 2: Knit the knit sts and purl the purl sts as they face you.
Repeat Row 2 for 3x1 Rib (worked flat).

BACK

Note: After the initial Provisional CO, use Backward Loop CO for any other COs in this pattern (see Special Techniques, page 152).

Using 32"-long circ needle, waste yarn and Provisional CO, CO 60 (64, 68, 72, 78, 82, 84) sts. (RS) Change to working yarn; begin St st. Work even until piece measures 6 (6½, 6½, 7¼, 7½, 7½, 8)" from the beginning, ending with a WS row.

Shape Armholes (RS): Increase 1 st each side this row, then every other row 1 (0, 1, 1, 2, 2, 2) time(s), as follows: K1, m1, work to last st, m1, k1—64 (66, 72, 76, 84, 88, 90) sts. Work even for 1 row.

Next Row (RS): CO 2 (3, 3, 5, 5, 6, 7) sts at beginning of next 2 rows, then 0 (3, 4, 5, 5, 7, 9) sts at beginning of next 2 rows—68 (78, 86, 96, 104, 114, 122) sts. Transfer sts to waste yarn for Body.

FRONT

With RS facing, carefully unravel Provisional CO and place first and last 16 (18, 20, 20, 22, 22, 22) sts on 32" long circ needle for Fronts. Transfer remaining center 28 (28, 28, 32, 34, 38, 40) sts to waste yarn for Back neck. Place removable marker for top of shoulder. (RS) Working BOTH SIDES AT SAME TIME using separate balls of yarn, begin St st. Work even for 16 rows.

Note: Neck and armhole shaping will be worked at the same time; neck shaping will not be completed until after pieces are joined, and for some sizes, it will not be completed until after waist shaping has begun. Please read entire section through waist shaping before beginning.

Shape Neck (RS): Increase 1 st each neck edge this row, then every 6 (6, 6, 4, 4, 4, 4) rows 6 (6, 6, 8, 9, 11, 12) times, as follows: On Right Front, knit to last st, m1, k1; on Left Front, k1, m1, knit to end. AT THE SAME TIME, when piece measures same as for Back to beginning of armholes, shape armholes as for Back, ending with a WS row. Break yarn for Right Front.

BODY

Join Back and Fronts (RS): With RS facing, transfer Back sts, then Right Front sts to left-hand end of circ needle. Your sts should now be in the following order, from right to left, with RS facing: Left Front, Back, Right Front. Using yarn attached to Left Front, and continuing neck shaping, work across Left Front, pm for side, Back, pm for side, then Right Front. Continuing neck shaping, work even until piece measures 2 (2, 1½, 1¼, 1¾, 1¾, 1¼)" from underarm, ending with a WS row.

Shape Waist (RS): Continuing neck shaping if necessary, decrease 4 sts this row, then every 10 rows once, as follows: [Work to 3 sts before marker, ssk, k1, sm, k1, k2tog] twice, work to end—114 (134, 150, 170, 186, 206, 222) sts remain when all shaping is complete. Work even for 1 row, decrease 3 sts at center Back—111 (131, 147, 167, 183, 203, 219) sts remain. Change to 3x1 Rib (worked flat); work even until piece measures 15 (15, 14½, 14¼, 14¾, 14¾, 14¼)" from underarm, ending with a WS row. BO all sts loosely in pattern.

SLEEVES

Note: Use your preferred method of working in the rnd when working the Sleeves (see page 23). You will be using 3 different color markers: 1 color for beginning of rnd, 2 of color A to mark end of cap shaping, and 2 of color B to mark center of cap shaping.

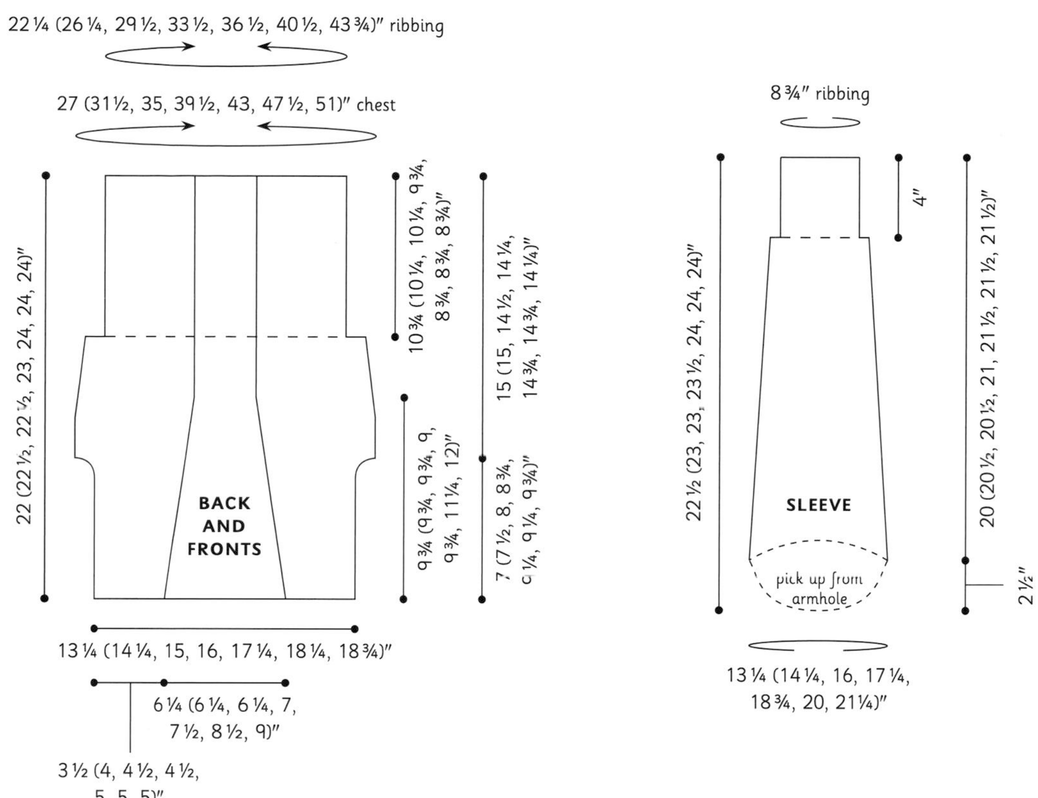

With RS facing, beginning at bottom center of underarm, pick up and knit 60 (64, 72, 78, 84, 90, 96) sts as follows: 7 (8, 11, 13, 15, 17, 19) sts, pm color A, 13 sts, pm color B, 20 (22, 24, 26, 28, 30, 32) sts, pm color B, 13 sts, pm color A, 7 (8, 11, 13, 15, 17, 19) sts. *Note: Be sure to pick up the same number of sts between bottom center of armhole and top of shoulder on both sides of the armhole. Color B markers should be equidistant from top of shoulder. If you would prefer not to place markers while you pick up sts, you may first pick up the total number of sts required, join for working in the rnd, then knit 1 rnd, placing the markers according to the numbers given in the pick-up instructions.*

Shape Cap

Note: Cap will be shaped using Short Rows (see Special Techniques, page 156). Hide wraps as you come to them.

Row 1: Working back and forth, begin St st. Work to second color B marker, sm, wrp-t.

Row 2: Repeat Row 1.

Row 3: Work to wrapped st of row before last row worked, work wrapped st, work 1 st, wrp-t.

Repeat Row 3 until you have reached the color A markers on each side of Sleeve.

Next Rnd (RS): Change to working in the rnd, hiding remaining wrap as you come to it, and removing all markers; pm for beginning of rnd. Work even for 6 rnds.

Shape Sleeve: Decrease 2 sts this rnd, every 11 (9, 6, 5, 5, 4, 4) rnds 3 (3, 10, 14, 5, 15, 6) times, then every 10 (8, 5, 4, 4, 3, 3) rnds 4 (6, 3, 2, 14, 7, 19) times as follows: K1, k2tog, work to last 3 sts, ssk, k1—44 sts remain. Work even until piece measures 16 (16½, 16½, 17, 17½, 17½, 17½)", measuring from bottom center of underarm, or to 4" from desired length. Change to 3x1 Rib (worked in the rnd). Work even for 4". BO all sts loosely in pattern.

Dexter
Washer Instructions
For Best Results
Maxi Load
Mega Load
3. Select wash cycle.
4. Insert coins to start washer.
LARGE WASHERS REQUIRE LESS
PLEASE DON'T OVERSUDS
Welcome...
BUT PLEASE BE ALERT
MACHINE PROBLEMS
Please Fill Out A Refund Card & Leave As Directed
USE CAUTION
Floors May Be Slippery Or Wet
SOAP
BLEACH
SOFTENERS
TRIPLE LOAD
DEXTER

FINISHING

Hood: Transfer Back neck sts from waste yarn to left-hand end of larger circ needle. With RS facing, beginning 10 rows below Right Front shoulder, pick up and knit 10 sts to shoulder, knit across half of Back neck sts, pm, knit to end, pick up and knit 10 sts from 10 rows below Left Front shoulder—48 (48, 48, 52, 54, 58, 60) sts. Working back and forth, begin St st; work even until piece measures 9" from pick-up row, ending with a WS row.

Shape Hood (RS): Increase 1 st each neck edge and decrease 2 sts at center back this row, then every other row 8 times, as follows: K1, m1, knit to 3 sts before center marker, ssk, k1, sm, k1, k2tog, work to last st, m1, k1. Work even for 1 row. Fold Hood in half and graft halves together using Kitchener st (see Special Techniques, page 152). If you prefer, you may BO all sts and sew the halves together, or use Three-Needle BO (see Special Techniques, page 153) to BO the sts.

Neck and Hood Edging: With RS facing, using 32"-long or longer circ needle, and beginning at bottom Right Front neck edge, pick up and knit a multiple of 4 sts + 3 along Right Front, Hood, and Left Front edges. Begin 3x1 Rib (worked flat); work even until piece measures 3" from pick-up row, ending with a WS row. BO all sts in pattern.

Block as desired. Sew eye to RS of Left Front, just above Body ribbing, approximately 1" in from pick-up row of Neck and Hood Edging. Sew hook to WS of Right Front, approximately 1" in from pick-up edge. Sew button to Left Front, adjacent to hook and centered on change from St st to ribbing on Body. *Note: For best results, try on for button placement.* Fold ribbon in half and sew ends to WS of Right Front Neck and Hood Edging, sewing it at both pick-up row and BO edge for added stability.

MAKE IT YOUR OWN

If you don't want to add a hood to your sweater, you can skip it altogether. And since the hood is added at the very end, you can put off your decision to-hood or not-to-hood until you work the edging. Here's how: When you pick up stitches for the ribbing along the fronts, start at one front edge and pick up the stitches along it, but continue picking up stitches along the shoulder, the back, and down the other front. After that, turn and follow the instructions as if you were working the ribbing around the hood, but knit the ribbing along the back instead. Be sure that when you pick up and knit stitches, you have the correct multiple of stitches so that it matches that of the ribbing. If you're extra adventurous, add some short rows between the two shoulder fronts to give a little lift along the back neck.

RIBBON

This versatile shell looks great on its own or under a blazer for days when you want a little more coverage. Worked in one piece, it's a quick knit, and the fun stitch pattern keeps things interesting. Note that the Stockinette stitch band along the sides allows you to shape the garment as much as you want without interrupting the ribbon motif.

PATTERN FEATURES

Top-down construction, twisted stitch pattern, simple shaping, crochet edging.

SIZES

X-Small (Small, Medium, Large, 1X-Large, 2X-Large, 3X-Large)

FINISHED MEASUREMENTS

29¾ (32¾, 36¼, 38½, 43, 46½, 50¼)" chest

YARN

Rowan Yarns Lenpur Linen (75% VI lenpur / 25% linen; 126 yards / 50 grams): 5 (5, 6, 7, 8, 8, 9) skeins #566 Tattoo

NEEDLES

One 32" (80 cm) long or longer circular (circ) needle size US 6 (4 mm)

One 16" (40 cm) long circular needle size US 5 (3.75 mm)

Change needle size if necessary to obtain correct gauge.

NOTIONS

Crochet hook size US G/6 (4 mm); waste yarn; stitch markers

GAUGE

22 sts and 28 rows = 4" (10 cm) in Zigzag Ribbon Stitch, using larger needle

ABBREVIATIONS

LI (lifted increase): Insert right-hand needle into the front of the st in the row below the next st on the left-hand needle; knit the st, then knit the next st on the needle.

BLI (back lifted increase): Insert right-hand needle from top down into the back of the st in the row below the next st on the left-hand needle; knit the st, then knit the next st on the needle.

STITCH PATTERNS

Zigzag Ribbon Stitch (worked flat)
(multiple of 10 sts; 24-row repeat)
Row 1 (WS) and all WS Rows: Purl.
Row 2: *L1, k2, ssk, k5; repeat from * to end.
Row 4: K1, *L1, k2, ssk, k5; repeat from * to last 9 sts, L1, k2, ssk, k4.
Row 6: K2, *L1, k2, ssk, k5; repeat from * to last 8 sts, L1, k2, ssk, k3.
Row 8: K3, *L1, k2, ssk, k5; repeat from * to last 7 sts, L1, k2, ssk, k2.
Row 10: K4, *L1, k2, ssk, k5; repeat from * to last 6 sts, L1, k2, ssk, k1.
Row 12: *K5, L1, k2, ssk; repeat from * to end.
Row 14: *K5, k2tog, k2, BLI; repeat from * to end.
Row 16: K4, *k2tog, k2, BLI, k5; repeat from * to last 6 sts, k2tog, k2, BLI, k1.
Row 18: K3, *k2tog, k2, BLI, k5; repeat from * to last 7 sts, k2tog, k2, BLI, k2.
Row 20: K2, *k2tog, k2, BLI, k5; repeat from * to last 8 sts, k2tog, k2, BLI, k3.
Row 22: K1, *k2tog, k2, BLI, k5; repeat from * to last 9 sts, k2tog, k2, BLI, k4.
Row 24: *K2tog, k2, BLI, k5; repeat from * to end.
Repeat Rows 1–24 for Zigzag Ribbon Stitch (worked flat).

Zigzag Ribbon Stitch (worked in the rnd)
(multiple of 10 sts; 24-rnd repeat)
Rnd 1 and all Odd-Numbered Rnds: Knit.
Rnd 2 and all Even-Numbered Rnds through Rnd 24: Work as for Zigzag Ribbon Stitch (worked flat).
Repeat Rnds 1–24 for Zigzag Ribbon Stitch (worked in the rnd).

Crab Stitch Edging
Row 1 (Single Crochet): Work from right to left for right-handers, or from left to right for left-handers. Make a slipknot and place on hook. *Insert hook into next st (along lower or upper edge) or between two rows (side edges). Yo hook, pull through to RS—2 loops on hook. Yo hook, draw through both loops—1 loop on hook. Repeat from * to end. *Note: It may be necessary to skip a row every so often when working along a side edge, in order to prevent puckering.*
Row 2 (Reverse Single Crochet): Work from left to right for right-handers, or from right to left for left-handers. *Insert hook into previous single crochet, yo hook, pull through to RS—2 loops on hook. Yo hook, draw through both loops—1 loop on hook. Repeat from * to end. Fasten off.

BACK

Note: When increasing or casting on sts, work new sts in St st.

Using larger needle, CO 72 (72, 82, 82, 92, 92, 102) sts.

Next Row (WS): Slip 1 (edge st), work Zigzag Ribbon Stitch (worked flat) to last st, p1 (edge st). Work even, slipping the first st of every row and working the last st of every row in St st, until piece measures 5¾ (5¾, 5¾, 6, 6¼, 6½, 6¾)" from the beginning, ending with a WS row. Make note of the row number of the pattern on which you ended.

Shape Armholes (RS): Working increased sts in St st as they become available, increase 1 st each side this row, then every other row 0 (1, 1, 2, 1, 1, 1) time(s), as follows: K1, m1, work to last st, m1, k1—74 (76, 86, 88, 96, 96, 106) sts. Work even for 1 row.

Next Row (RS): CO 2 (3, 3, 4, 3, 3, 3) sts at beginning of next 2 rows, 2 (4, 4, 5, 3, 5, 5) sts at beginning of next 2 rows, then 0 (0, 0, 0, 5, 8, 8) sts at beginning of next 2 rows—82 (90, 100, 106, 118, 128, 138) sts. Transfer sts to waste yarn for Body.

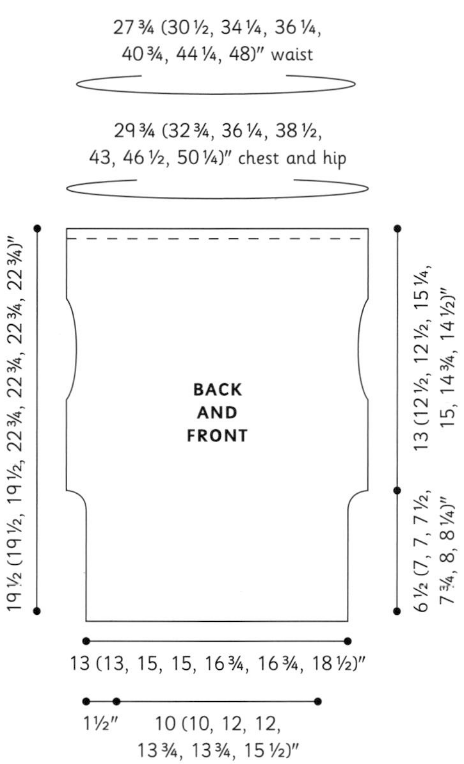

FRONT

Work as for Back; do not transfer sts to waste yarn.

BODY

Join Back and Front (RS): With RS of Back and Front facing, transfer sts for Back to left-hand end of needle. Beginning with row following last row worked in pattern, work patterns as established across Front sts, pm for side, work across Back sts—164 (180, 200, 212, 236, 256, 276) sts. Join for working in the rnd; pm for beginning of rnd. Beginning with rnd following last row worked in pattern, begin Zigzag Ribbon Stitch (worked in the rnd); work even until piece measures 4 ½ (4 ½, 5, 5 ½, 5 ¾, 5 ½, 6 ¼)" from underarm.

Shape Waist: Decrease 4 sts this rnd, then every 7 rnds twice, as follows: [K1, k2tog, work to 3 sts before marker, ssk, k1, sm] twice—152 (168, 188, 200, 224, 244, 264) sts remain. Work even for 6 rnds.

Shape Hip: Increase 4 sts this rnd, then every 7 rnds, as follows: [K1, m1, work to 1 st before marker, m1, k1, sm] twice—164 (180, 200, 212, 236, 256, 276) sts. Work even until piece measures approximately 12 ½ (12, 12, 14 ¾, 14 ½, 14 ¼, 14)" from underarm, ending with Rnd 12 or 24 of pattern. Change to Garter st (knit 1 rnd, purl 1 rnd); work even for 5 rnds. BO all sts loosely purlwise.

FINISHING

Sew shoulder seam for approximately 1 ½" in from each armhole edge, or to desired shoulder width.

Armhole Edging: Using crochet hook, beginning at bottom center of armhole, work Crab Stitch Edging around armhole. For a tighter fitting armhole, instead of working Crab Stitch Edging, work as follows: *Single crochet, sl st; repeat from * to end.

Block as desired.

MAKE IT YOUR OWN

It's easy to add little capped sleeves—or sleeves of any length—by following the Afterthought Sleeves instructions on page 23. For more guidance on how to work capped sleeves, check out Blithe Tee on page 78.

KNOTTED

This vest is the perfect trans-seasonal garment to throw on while you're running out the door. Knit with a tone-on-tone dk weight yarn, the subtle variations in color give the simple Stockinette canvas a little depth and interest. The sample shown here has just one closure on the front and some ribbon sewn to the inside edging for stabilization. Ideas for variations are given on page 40.

BACK

Note: After the initial Provisional CO, use Backward Loop CO for any other COs in this pattern (see Special Techniques, page 152). Using larger circ needle, waste yarn and Provisional CO, CO 64 (66, 70, 72, 76, 78, 84) sts. (RS) Change to working yarn; begin St st. Work even until piece measures 6½ (6¾, 7½, 8, 8¼, 8¼, 8½)" from the beginning, ending with a WS row.

Shape Armholes (RS): Increase 1 st each side this row, then every other row 1 (1, 1, 2, 2, 3, 3) time(s), as follows: K1, m1, work to last st, m1, k1—68 (70, 74, 78, 82, 86, 92) sts. Work even for 1 row.

Next Row (RS): CO 3 (4, 6, 7, 8, 10, 11) sts at beginning of next 2 rows, then 5 (6, 8, 8, 9, 12, 13) sts at beginning of next 2 rows—84 (90, 102, 108, 116, 130, 140) sts. Transfer sts to waste yarn for Body.

FRONT

With RS facing, carefully unravel Provisional CO and place first and last 15 (15, 17, 17, 19, 21, 23) sts on larger circ needle for Fronts. Transfer remaining center 34 (36, 36, 38, 38, 36, 38) sts to waste yarn for Back neck. Place removable marker for top of shoulder. (RS) Working BOTH SIDES AT SAME TIME using separate balls

PATTERN FEATURES

Top-down construction, provisional cast-on, simple stitch pattern, simple shaping, short-row shaping (hooded variation), picking up and knitting, ribbing.

SIZES

X-Small (Small, Medium, Large, 1X-Large, 2X-Large, 3X-Large)

FINISHED MEASUREMENTS

31½ (33¼, 37¾, 40¼, 43¼, 48¾, 52)" chest, including Front Bands

YARN

Lorna's Laces Green Line DK (100% organic merino wool; 145 yards / 2 ounces): 5 (6, 6, 6, 7, 8, 8) hanks Butterscotch (sleeveless version) or 7 (8, 9, 9, 10, 11, 11) hanks Chagrin (hooded variation)

NEEDLES

One 32" (80 cm) long or longer circular (circ) needle sizes US 6 (4 mm) and US 5 (3.75 mm)

One 16" (40 cm) long circular needle size US 5 (3.75 mm) (Sleeveless Version only)

One or two 24" (60 cm) long or longer circular needles or one set of five double-pointed needles (dpn) sizes US 6 (4 mm) and US 5 (3.75 mm), as preferred, for Sleeves (Hooded Variation only)

Change needle size if necessary to obtain correct gauge.

NOTIONS

Waste yarn; removable marker; stitch markers in 3 colors; 2 yards ⅝"-wide grosgrain ribbon; sewing needle and matching thread; 1 extra-large hook and eye

GAUGE

22 sts and 28 rows = 4" (10 cm) in Stockinette stitch (St st), using larger needles

STITCH PATTERNS

Knotted Rib Stitch (worked flat)
(odd number of sts; 6-row repeat)
Row 1 (RS): P1, *k1-f/b/f, p1; repeat from * to end—2 sts increased.
Row 2: K1, *p3tog, k1; repeat from * to end—2 sts decreased.
Rows 3 and 5: P1, *k1, p1; repeat from * to end.
Rows 4 and 6: K1, *p1, k1; repeat from * to end.
Repeat Rows 1–6 for Knotted Rib Stitch (worked flat).

Knotted Rib Stitch (worked in the rnd)
(even number of sts; 6-rnd repeat)
Rnd 1: *P1, k1-f/b/f; repeat from * to end—2 sts increased.
Rnd 2: *P1, k3tog, repeat from * to end—2 sts decreased.
Rnds 3–6: *P1, k1; repeat from * to end.
Repeat Rnds 1–6 for Knotted Rib Stitch (worked in the rnd).

1x1 Rib (worked flat)
(odd number of sts; 2-rnd repeat)
Row 1 (RS): K1, *p1, k1; repeat from * to end.
Row 2: P1, *k1, p1; repeat from * to end.
Repeat Rows 1 and 2 for 1x1 Rib (worked flat).

1x1 Rib (worked in the rnd)
(even number of sts; 1-rnd repeat)
All Rnds: *K1, p1; repeat from * to end.

of yarn, begin St st; work even for 12 rows. Change to Knotted Rib Stitch (worked flat); work Rows 1–6 twice, then Rows 1 and 2 once. Knit 1 row. Purl 1 row.

Shape Neck (RS): *Note: Neck and armhole shaping are worked at the same time; please read entire section through before beginning.* Increase 1 st each neck edge this row, every 4 rows 3 times, then every other row 5 times, as follows: On Right Front, work to last st, m1, k1; on Left Front, k1, m1, work to end. Work even for 1 row.

Next Row (RS): CO 4 sts at each neck edge once, then 4 (4, 4, 6, 6, 6, 6) sts once. AT THE SAME TIME, when piece measures same as for Back from top of shoulder to beginning of armhole shaping, shape armhole as for Back, ending with a WS row. *Note: Some sizes may not complete the neck shaping until after the Fronts and Back are joined.* Break yarn for Right Front.

BODY

Join Back to Fronts

With RS facing, transfer Back sts, then Right Front sts to left-hand end of circ needle. *Note: The Back sts referred to are the sts that were placed on waste yarn after working the armhole shaping, not the Back neck sts that were placed on waste yarn after unraveling the Provisional CO.* Your sts should now be in the following order, from right to left, with RS facing: Left Front, Back, Right Front. Using yarn attached to Left Front, and continuing with neck shaping if necessary, work across Left Front, pm for left side, work across Back, pm for right side, work across Right Front—168 (178, 202, 216, 232, 262, 280) sts when all shaping is complete. Working back and forth, work even until piece measures 12½ (13, 13½, 14, 14½, 14½, 14¾)" from the beginning, ending with a RS row.

Next Row (WS): Work to 21 (23, 26, 27, 29, 32, 35) sts past first marker, pm for back waist shaping, work 42 (44, 50, 54, 58, 66, 70) sts, pm for back waist shaping, work to end.

Shape Back Waist (RS): *Note: Shaping occurs on Back only; Fronts are not shaped.* Decrease 2 sts this row, then every 6 rows twice, as follows: Work to second marker, sm, k2tog, work to 2 sts before next marker, ssk, sm, work to end—162 (172, 196, 210, 226, 256, 274) sts remain; 78 (84, 96, 102, 110, 124, 134) sts for Back. Work even for 5 rows.

Next Row (RS): Increase 2 sts this row, then every 6 rows twice, as follows: Work to second marker, sm, m1, work to next marker, m1, sm, work to end—168 (178, 202, 216, 232, 262, 280) sts; 84 (90, 102, 108, 116, 130, 140) sts for Back. Work even until piece measures 22 (24, 24, 24, 25, 25, 25)" from the beginning, ending with a WS row, increase 1 st on last row—169 (179, 203, 217, 233, 263, 281) sts. Change to smaller circ needle and 1x1 Rib (worked flat); work even for 4 rows. BO all sts loosely in pattern.

POCKET

Using smaller circ needle, CO 25 (25, 25, 25, 29, 29, 29) sts. Begin St st; work even for 5 rows.

Turning Row (RS): *K1-tbl; repeat from * to end. Purl 1 row.

Next Row (RS): Change to larger needles. Continuing in St st, CO 2 sts at beginning and end of row—29 (29, 29, 29, 33, 33, 33) sts. Work even until piece measures 2" from Turning Row, slipping the first st of every row, and ending with a WS row.

Next Row (RS): Slip 1, work in Knotted Rib Stitch (worked flat) to last st, k1. Work even, working Rows 1–6 of Knotted Rib Stitch twice, then Rows 1 and 2 twice, slipping the first st of every row and working the last st of every row in St st, and working Knotted Rib Stitch on center 27 (27, 27, 27, 31, 31, 31) sts. BO all sts loosely knitwise.

SLEEVES (for Hooded Variation only)

Note: Use your preferred method of working in the rnd when working the Sleeves (see page 23). You will be using 3 different color markers: one color for beginning of rnd, 2 of color A to mark end of cap shaping, and 2 of color B to mark center of cap shaping.

With RS facing, beginning at bottom center of underarm, using larger needle(s), pick up and knit 76 (80, 86, 92, 100, 106, 106) sts as follows: 9 (10, 12, 14, 14, 16, 16) sts, pm color A, 17 (17, 17, 17, 19, 19, 19) sts, pm color B, 24 (26, 28, 30, 34, 36, 36) sts, pm color B, 17 (17, 17, 17, 19, 19, 19) sts, pm color A, 9 (10, 12, 14, 14, 16, 16) sts. *Note: Be sure to pick up the same number of sts between bottom center of armhole and top of shoulder on both sides of the armhole. Color B markers should be equidistant from top of shoulder. If you would prefer not to place markers while you pick up sts, you may first pick up the total number of sts required, join for working in the rnd, then knit 1 rnd, placing the markers according to the numbers given in the pick-up instructions.*

Shape Cap

Note: Cap will be shaped using Short Rows (see Special Techniques, page 156). Hide wraps as you come to them.

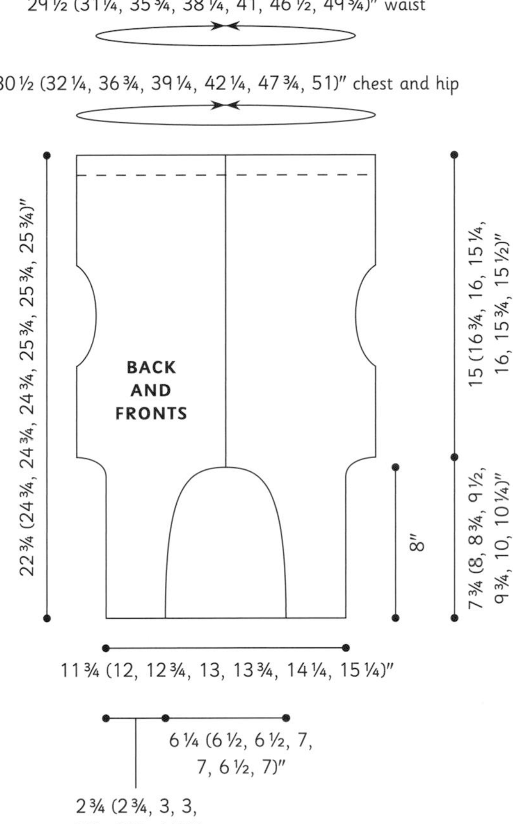

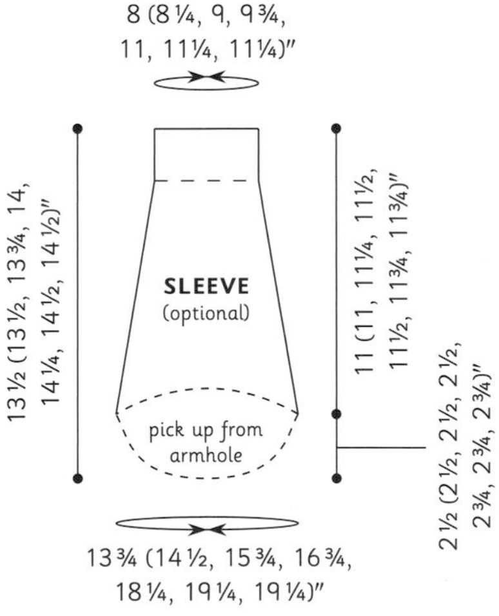

Row 1: Working back and forth, begin St st, work to second color B marker, sm, wrp-t.

Row 2: Repeat Row 1.

Row 3: Work to wrapped st of row below last row worked, work wrapped st, work 1 st, wrp-t.

Repeat Row 3 until you have reached the color A markers on each side of the Sleeve.

Next Rnd (RS): Change to working in the rnd, hiding remaining wrap as you come to it, and removing all markers; pm for beginning of rnd. Work even for 3 rnds.

Shape Sleeve: Decrease 2 sts this rnd, then every 3 rnds 15 (16, 17, 18, 19, 21, 21) times, as follows: K1, k2tog, work to last 3 sts, ssk, k1—44 (46, 50, 54, 60, 62, 62) sts remain. Work even until piece measures 8¾ (8¾, 9, 9¼, 9¼, 10, 10)" measuring from bottom center of underarm, or to 2¼" from desired length.

Next Rnd: Change to smaller needles and Knotted Rib Stitch (worked in the rnd); work Rnds 1–6 twice, then Rnds 1 and 2 once. BO all sts loosely in pattern, working Rnd 3 of pattern as you BO.

FINISHING

Sleeveless Version

Armholes: With RS facing, using smaller 16" circ needle, beginning at bottom center of underarm, pick up and knit approximately 1 st for every BO st and 3 sts for every 4 rows around the armhole, making sure to end with an even number of sts. Join for working in the rnd; pm for beginning of rnd. Begin 1x1 Rib (worked in the rnd); work even for 4 rnds. BO all sts loosely in pattern.

Neckband: Transfer Back neck sts from waste yarn to left-hand end of smaller circ needle. With RS facing, beginning at Right Front neck edge, pick up and knit 1 st for every BO st and approximately 3 sts for every 4 rows to the Back neck sts, making sure to end with an even number of sts; work 1x1 Rib (worked flat) across Back neck sts. Pick up and knit an odd number of sts to Left Front neck edge. (WS) Begin 1x1 Rib (worked flat); work even for 4 rows. BO all sts loosely in pattern.

Front Bands: With RS facing, using smaller 32"-long circ needle, pick up and knit approximately 3 sts for every 4 rows along Right Front edge, ending with an odd number of sts. (WS) Begin 1x1 Rib (worked flat); work even for 4 rows. BO all sts loosely in pattern.

Cut 2 lengths of ribbon long enough to fit Front Bands, plus ¼" at each end for finishing. Using sewing thread, sew ribbon to WS of Left Front Band, folding ¼" of ribbon to WS at each end for a neat edge. Repeat for Right Front Band. Sew hook on Right Front Band, ½" below Neckband. Sew eye on Left Front Band, opposite hook.

Fold hem of Pocket to WS at Turning Row. Sew pocket to lower Right Front (see photo), sewing bottom edge at Turning Row.

Block as desired.

Hooded Variation

Hood: Transfer Back neck sts from waste yarn to left-hand end of larger circ needle. With RS facing, using larger circ needle, and beginning 10 rows below Right Front shoulder, pick up and knit 10 sts to shoulder, knit across half of Back neck sts, pm, knit to end, pick up and knit 10 sts from 10 rows below Left Front shoulder—54 (56, 56, 58, 58, 56, 58) sts. Working back and forth, begin St st; work even until piece measures 9" from pick-up row, ending with a WS row.

Shape Hood (RS): Increase 1 st each neck edge and decrease 2 sts at center back this row, then every other row 9 times, as follows: K1, m1, knit to 3 sts before center marker, ssk, k1, sm, k1, k2tog, work to last st, m1, k1. Work even for 1 row. Fold Hood in half and graft halves together using Kitchener st (see Special Techniques, page 152). If you prefer, you may BO all sts and sew the halves together, or use Three-Needle BO (see Special Techniques, page 153) to BO the sts.

Neck and Hood Edging: With RS facing, using smaller needles and beginning at Right Front neck shaping, pick up and knit 1 st for every BO st and approximately 3 sts for every 4 rows along neck edge, making sure to end with an odd number of sts. (WS) Begin 1x1 Rib (worked flat); work even for 4 rows. BO all sts loosely in pattern. Complete as for Sleeveless Version, beginning with Front Bands.

MAKE IT YOUR OWN

This red version of Knotted is similar to the original on page 36 except I added a hood and Afterthought Sleeves. To do either, the only skills you need are the ability to pick up and knit around the shoulders and back areas; of course, you also need to have enough yarn on hand to add these elements. See page 22 for more information on adding a hood or sleeves, or use this pattern for step-by-step guidance. Other variations you might want to try are adjusting length, adding a zipper, or sewing ribbon to the outside of the Left Front and adding snaps.

SIZES

X-Small (Small, Medium, Large, 1X-Large, 2X-Large, 3X-Large)

FINISHED MEASUREMENTS

32 (35¼, 38½, 41½, 44¾, 48, 51¼)"

YARN

Mirasol Tupa (50% merino wool / 50% silk; 137 yards / 50 grams): 8 (9, 9, 10, 10, 11, 12) hanks #806 Rose Quartz

NEEDLES

One 32" (80 cm) long or longer circular (circ) needle size US 6 (4 mm)

One 16" (40 cm) long circular needle size US 6 (4 mm)

One 16" (40 cm) long circular needle size US 7 (4.5 mm)

Change needle size if necessary to obtain correct gauge.

NOTIONS

Waste yarn; removable stitch marker; stitch markers

GAUGE

20 sts and 24 rows = 4" (10 cm) in Diamond Seed Brocade, using smaller needle

BIJOU

Given that I live in Southern California, I almost never need anything that will keep me too warm, so this top-down, simply constructed cowl pullover is perfect for me. Throw on a low-slung belt, leggings, and some strappy sandals for a chic warmer-weather look.

PATTERN FEATURES

Top down construction, provisional cast-on, simple stitch pattern, picking up and knitting, ribbing.

STITCH PATTERNS

Diamond Seed Brocade (worked flat)
(multiple of 8 sts; 8-row repeat)
Row 1 (RS): *P1, k7; repeat from * to end.
Row 2: *K1, p5, k1, p1; repeat from * to end.
Rows 3 and 7: *K2, p1, k3, p1, k1; repeat from * to end.
Rows 4 and 6: *P2, k1, p1, k1, p3; repeat from * to end.
Row 5: *K4, p1, k3; repeat from * to end.
Row 8: Repeat Row 2.
Repeat Rows 1–8 for Diamond Seed Brocade.

Diamond Seed Brocade (worked in the rnd)
(multiple of 8 sts; 8-rnd repeat)
Rnd 1: *P1, k7; repeat from * to end.
Rnd 2: *K1, p1, k5, p1; repeat from * to end.
Rnds 3 and 7: *K2, p1, k3, p1, k1; repeat from * to end.
Rnds 4 and 6: *K3, p1, k1, p1, k2; repeat from * to end.
Rnd 5: *K4, p1, k3; repeat from * to end.
Rnd 8: Repeat Rnd 2.
Repeat Rnds 1–8 for Diamond Seed Brocade.

1x1 Rib
(multiple of 2 sts; 1-rnd repeat)
All Rnds: *K1, p1; repeat from * to end.

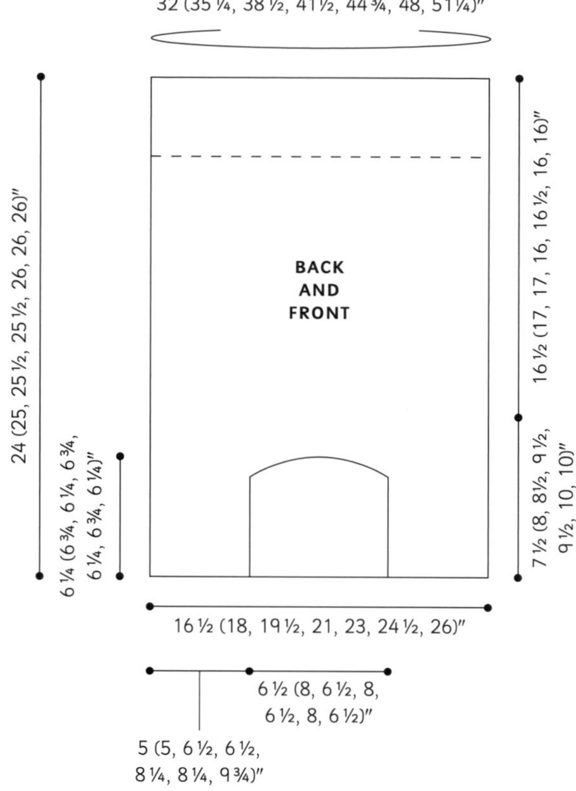

BACK

Note: After the initial Provisional CO, use Backward Loop CO for any other COs in this pattern (see Special Techniques, page 152).

Using 32" circ needle, waste yarn and Provisional CO, CO 82 (90, 98, 106, 114, 122, 130) sts. (RS) Change to working yarn. Begin St st; work even for 2 rows.

Next Row (RS): K1 (edge st, keep in St st), work Diamond Seed Brocade (worked flat) to last st, k1 (edge st, keep in St st). Work even until piece measures 7 ½ (8, 8 ½, 9 ½, 9 ½, 10, 10)" from the beginning, ending with a WS row. Make note of last pattern row worked. Transfer sts to waste yarn for Body.

FRONT

With RS facing, carefully unravel Provisional CO and place first and last 25 (25, 33, 33, 41, 41, 49) sts on 32" circ needle for Fronts. Transfer remaining center 32 (40, 32, 40, 32, 40, 32) sts to waste yarn for Back neck. Place removable marker for top of shoulder. (RS) Working BOTH SIDES AT SAME TIME, using separate balls of yarn and keeping armhole edge sts in St st as for Back, begin Diamond Seed Brocade (worked flat); work even until piece measures 5" from top of shoulder, ending with a WS row.

Shape Neck (RS): CO 4 sts at each neck edge every other row 3 (4, 3, 4, 3, 4, 3) times—37 (41, 45, 49, 53, 57, 61) st each side. Work even for 1 row.

Join Fronts (RS): Work across Right Front, CO 8 sts for center neck, work across Left Front to end, cutting second ball of yarn—82 (90, 98, 106, 114, 122, 130) sts. Work even until piece measures same as for Back from top of shoulder, ending with same row of pattern as for Back.

BODY

Join Back and Front (RS): Change to Diamond Seed Brocade (worked in the rnd), beginning with rnd following last row worked and, at the same time, decrease 4 sts as follows: Work 2 sts together, work across Front sts to last 2 sts, work 2 sts together; working across Back sts from waste yarn, work 2 sts together, work across Back sts to last 2 sts, work 2 sts together. Join for working in the rnd; pm for beginning of rnd—160 (176, 192, 208, 224, 240, 256) sts. *Note: The Back sts referred to are the sts that were placed on waste yarn after working the Back, not the Back neck sts that were placed on waste yarn after unraveling the Provisional CO.* Work even until piece measures 20 (21, 21½, 21½, 22, 22, 22)" from top of shoulder. Change to 1x1 Rib; work even for 4". BO all sts loosely in pattern.

FINISHING

Collar: Place Back neck sts on smaller 16" circ needle. With RS facing, and with Back neck sts at right-hand end of circ needle, pick up and knit an even number of sts around neck opening. Join for working in the rnd; pm for beginning of rnd. Begin 1x1 Rib; work even for 3". Change to larger 16" circ needle; work even until piece measures 9" from pick-up rnd. BO all sts loosely in pattern.

Armhole Edging: With RS facing, using smaller 16" circ needle, beginning at center underarm, pick up and knit approximately 1 st for every CO st and 3 sts for every 4 rows around armhole, making sure to end with an even number of sts. Join for working in the rnd; pm for beginning of rnd. Begin 1x1 Rib; work even for 1½". BO all sts loosely in pattern.

Block as desired.

MAKE IT YOUR OWN

If you want to make this a warmer sweater, add long sleeves. To do this, skip the ribbing at the armholes, pick up and knit stitches in the correct multiple for the stitch pattern, and work the sleeves down toward the cuff, adding sleeve shaping if desired (see Afterthought Sleeves, page 23). Instead of the cowl, you could make a wide neck and wear it off the shoulder by picking up stitches around the neckline and working a similar edging to the sleeve and hem. You could also stop working the Body above the waist and work ribbing for several inches for a more fitted look.

CHAPTER 3

He Said, She Said: Converting Patterns to Fit Men, Women, and Children

Many times we look at a knitting pattern and wonder why it isn't sized for everyone in the family. Or maybe we find something that would look good on so-and-so, but he's a guy and this is a woman's pattern. Believe it or not, a knitting pattern can be adapted to work on almost anyone, whatever shape, size, gender, or age, and in this chapter I show you how.

ONE PATTERN, MANY PEOPLE

Whether it started out as a pattern for a man or a woman, a little girl or boy, once you have your measurements on hand, you can upsize or downsize it, retaining elements of its original look and doing away with elements that don't work.

In order to deconstruct a sweater pattern and rebuild it to suit your needs, you first need to understand exactly how it was constructed. Top-down raglans are usually great patterns to convert since they begin with a basic measurement—the back neck—and are created by

Standard Measurements Comparison Chart

Child's Sizes	TWO	FOUR	SIX	EIGHT	TEN
Chest:	21″	23″	25″	26½″	28″
Back Waist:	8½″	9½″	10½″	12½″	14″
Crossback:	9¼″	9¾″	10¼″	10¾″	11¼″
Sleeve Length*:	8½″	10½″	11½″	12½″	13½″

Women's Sizes	X-SMALL	SMALL	MEDIUM	LARGE	1X-LARGE	2X-LARGE	3X-LARGE	4X-LARGE	5X-LARGE
Chest:	28–30″	32–34″	36–38″	40–42″	44–46″	48–50″	52–54″	56–58″	60–62″
Back Waist:	16½″	17″	17¼″	17½″	17¾″	18″	18″	18½″	18½″
Crossback:	14–14½″	14½–15″	16–16½″	17–17½″	17½″	18″	18″	18½″	18½″
Sleeve Length*:	16½″	17″	17″	17½″	17½″	18″	18″	18½″	18½″

Men's Sizes	SMALL	MEDIUM	LARGE	X-LARGE	XX-LARGE
Chest:	34–36″	38–40″	42–44″	46–48″	50–52″
Back Hip Length:**	25–25½″	26½–26¾″	27–27¼″	27½–27¾″	28–28½″
Crossback:	15½–16″	16½–17″	17½–18″	18–18½″	18½–19″
Sleeve Length*:	18″	18½″	19½″	20″	20½″

*Measurement from underarm to wrist

**In men's sizes, because there isn't waist shaping, we use hip measurements to determine how long a garment should be.

FROM CRAFT YARN COUNCIL OF AMERICA "STANDARDS AND GUIDELINES FOR CROCHET AND KNITTING" adding increases at four key points. Because of their straightforward construction, raglans can be sized up or down for just about anybody by simply beginning with a stitch count that matches the measurement of the recipient's back neck and working until the yoke "fits." You can read through a raglan pattern like the Holden Jacket (page 54) to see how raglans are worked after you've cast on. If you're converting a child's or man's raglan to a woman's, you might want to adjust the raglan depth or add some body shaping (read more about tailoring raglans in chapter 4). Otherwise, that's about it.

With a top-down set-in sleeve garment, things are a bit different. These garments begin with a crossback measurement (narrower for set-in sleeves, wider for semi-dropped or dropped sleeves). From there, you'll need to consider the armhole depth, which directly correlates to the upper arm circumference when you add Afterthought Sleeves (see page 23).

No matter what type of pattern you want to make, it's always easiest to convert a basic pattern—one that doesn't feature things like allover cabling, tricky colorwork, or complicated shaping. The simpler the design, the less time you'll have to spend recentering cables or recalculating stitch counts for specialized stitch patterns. If you do want to convert a pattern with cables, stitch patterns, specific shaping, etc., make sure to look at it realistically to see if you can really make your downsized, upsized, or masculinized version an exact (or near) replica of the original for a different body type. One word of caution: If you find yourself changing so many elements in order to resize that you're practically redesigning the whole garment, it will probably be easier to bite the bullet and simply design the garment from scratch (see page 145) or go out and find another pattern close to what you're looking for.

When veering away from an existing pattern, it's optimal if the sweater recipient is available for try-ons. If not, it's helpful to have their measurements and one of their favorite well-fitting garments on hand so that you can hold it up to your knitting for comparison. And finally, any time you convert a pattern, check to make sure that you have the right amount of yarn (see page 15).

UPSIZED FROM A WOMAN'S PATTERN

SIZED FOR MOM AND DAUGHTER

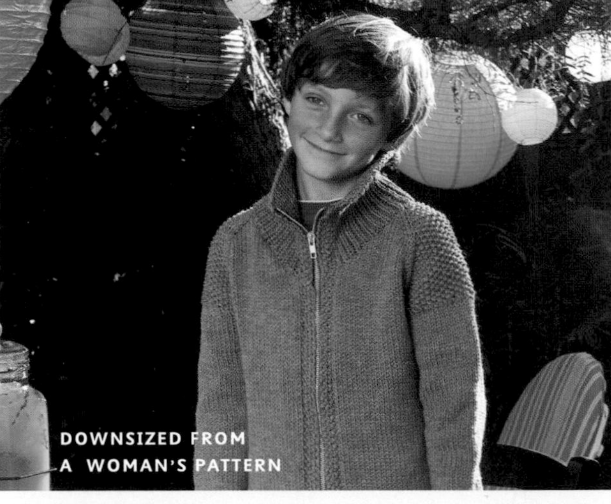

DOWNSIZED FROM A WOMAN'S PATTERN

Downsizing a Pattern

There are lots of situations when you might want to make a smaller version of a pattern. Maybe your daughter loves the sweater you made for yourself and wants one of her own. Or perhaps you're coveting a man's sweater pattern and want one in your size. Follow the steps below to downsize a top-down pattern.

1 Look at the pattern and determine what type it is. Is it a raglan or a set-in sleeve? When converting a raglan, you must take the back neck measurement of the person for whom you are knitting the sweater (there are no standard sizing charts for this particular measurement). When converting a set-in-sleeve garment, take note of the standard crossback measurement on the chart on page 48. Compare the recipient's measurements to the existing pattern. If there is not a size close enough to the one you want to make, consult the aforementioned sizing charts, refer back to the pattern, and decide on the closest size you can knit. Then adjust the number of stitches you cast on to fit your recipient's back neck (in the case of a raglan) or crossback measurement (in the case of the set-in sleeve). To get the proper number of stitches to cast on, multiply the back neck or crossback measurement by the stitch gauge of your yarn; make sure that you have enough stitches to accommodate the multiple of the stitch pattern you are working on. Chest circumference can more easily be dealt with later.

2 Plan ahead for your neckline shaping and make sure that the person's head can fit through the neck opening if you are making a pullover. Inspect the schematic for that information, and as you work from the top front down to your neckline shaping, make note of the depth of the neck to ensure that it won't be too low or too short. Since you're downsizing, you may decide to begin shaping and joining the two fronts before the pattern tells you to do so.

3 Look at the schematic for the armhole or yoke depth for your chosen size and decide, based on the sizing charts, if you need to SUBTRACT a little length. If you do, make notes in your pattern to work the armhole that much LESS before you begin armhole shaping in set-in-sleeve construction; raglans are just knit to the correct depth. See page 87 for tips on how to control the chest and sleeve circumferences in raglans.

4 Once you have completed the armholes and are working the body, look forward in the pattern to see if there is waist shaping. If the sweater is for a man or a child, you will very likely skip any waist shaping instructions and work straight through. If the sweater is for a woman but was originally written for a man, you may want to add some waist shaping (see page 21).

5 As you continue working toward the hem, decide if you will subtract length based on either your recipient's personal measurements or the sizing chart. Note that most schematics show measurements minus the trim (hems and cuffs do not count as trims, but necklines usually do).

6 Consider the ribbing and trims on your pattern. Do you want to subtract length from the ribbing on the hem and cuffs? If you want to change out the stitch pattern, make sure that you have the correct multiple of stitches on the needles before you get to that part of the sweater.

7 As you work your sleeves, if they are raglan, you can check your recipient's arm length (from underarm to wrist for a long sleeve), or look at the chart to decide if you want to work them to a shorter length before adding ribbing. If you are working an Afterthought Sleeve as for set-in sleeve construction, stitch counts will likely change because you may have opted to make a shorter armhole. If this is the case, see page 23 for information on refiguring the number of short rows and their placement in Afterthought Sleeves.

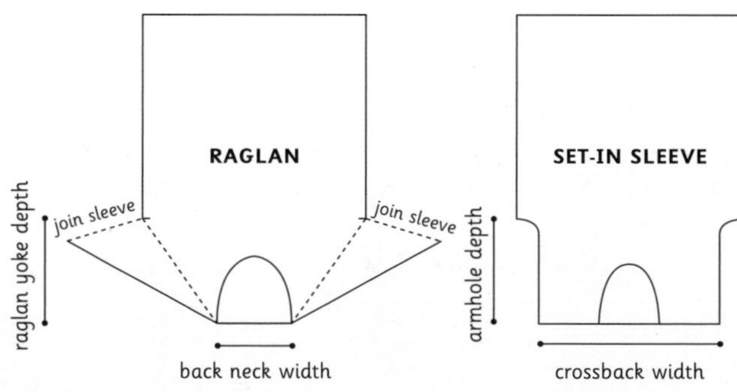

Reality Checklist: Important Points to Consider When Converting a Pattern

✦ Whether you're converting a woman's pattern to a man's pattern or the other way around, you'll need to consult the sizing charts on page 48 so that you can compare and contrast typical male and female sizes. Surprisingly, many women's patterns come in chest sizes that match those found in men's—and even boy's—patterns. But you'll also notice some basic differences between women's and men's sizing. For example, crossback measurements tend to be slightly wider for men and boys (especially in the smaller sizes), and their sleeve lengths and armholes are about an inch longer. Body length is usually longer, too, but not by as much as you would think. Your best bet, always, is trying on as you go or comparing your garment to a sample sweater that belongs to the recipient.

✦ The calculator is your friend. Use it often and keep notes of every stitch count at the important parts of your converted pattern. You might decide you like the result so much that you want to knit another one—then you won't have to do the math again.

✦ If you're converting a man's pattern to a woman's, keep track of ease. Men's patterns are typically meant to fit looser than women's, and if you follow a pattern that is sized for, say, "small, medium, large," etc., but it doesn't give finished measurements, then be sure to check the schematic. If there isn't one, spend a few moments checking stitch counts at key points and use your calculator to figure out what the true measurements will be before deciding on what size to knit for yourself. You might begin thinking you want a medium, and then look more closely and decide you need a small instead. You may also want to check the depth of the armholes and adjust them, too.

✦ Men probably won't want low V-necks, scoop necks, or sweetheart necklines. Ditto for boys.

✦ You'd be surprised by how large kids' heads are. By the time they're three or four years old, their heads are only an inch or two smaller than adult heads, coming in at about 18" around (an adult runs between 20" and 22"). When downsizing an adult pattern to a kid's pattern, especially a crewneck, be careful not to subtract more than a couple of inches in the final neck circumference.

✦ If the converted pattern is for a boy, a man, or even a child of either gender, you will very likely skip waist shaping instructions and work straight through. If the pattern is for a woman and was originally for a man or boy, you'll want to add waist shaping and maybe even short rows at the bust.

✦ Whenever you change the depth of an armhole, you will also be altering the total circumference of your sleeve at the upper arm. This will be true for both raglan and set-in sleeve constructions.

✦ Check the ribbings, edgings, and cables or any other motifs for age/gender appropriateness and adjust, if necessary. If you are starting out with a man's pattern and downsizing for a woman, for example, you might consider shortening cuffs and edgings so that the overall style is more feminine looking. Men and boys tend to need a more masculine balance of ribbing to Stockinette stitch than women and girls.

✦ Add Bobbles? Never.

Upsizing a Pattern

At some point you may find a kids' pattern so irresistible that you want to "upsize" it for yourself. Or maybe you've found the perfect sweater for your man, but it's written in women's sizes. If you're working from a raglan pattern, upsizing the pattern will be pretty straightforward: You just begin with the proper number of back neck stitches and a few for the sleeves and the fronts, then work the yoke, increasing along each side of each of your markers as directed in the pattern until the yoke "fits."

When upsizing a top-down set-in-sleeve sweater, or even a bottom-up pattern that's worked in pieces, you're essentially "borrowing" elements from the original pattern, like stitch patterns, stripes, motifs, and certain style elements like sleeve shaping, length, and neckline shaping. Other than these elements, you'll pretty much be writing your own pattern so it fits you.

Incidentally, the steps you need to follow to upsize a pattern are the very same steps you follow to convert a pattern that's worked in pieces to one that is top-down in the round. So this section is sort of a two-for-one deal! To convert either a top-down set-in-sleeve sweater or a bottom-up pieced sweater, begin by referring to a general sizing chart (or a size chart that you've made for yourself) and do some preplanning, like drawing a simple schematic and calculating how much yarn you will need (see page 15). Once you've plotted out these elements, you should end up with an upsized version of your favorite pattern without too much trouble. Here's a step-by-step breakdown of how to do it:

1 Write down the following measurements: Crossback, bust, armhole depth, and back of neck, or use measurements from the charts on page 48 that match your own.

2 Assuming the gauge you are using is the same as that in the pattern, calculate how many stitches you will cast on provisionally, compared to the original pattern. For example, if the stitch gauge in the pattern is 6 stitches to the inch and your own crossback measurement is 14″, you will cast on 84 stitches. Note that if there is a stitch pattern in your original pattern, you may need to adjust the number of cast-on stitches to accommodate the multiple. In other words, say the sweater has 2x2 ribbing throughout. When worked flat, this requires a multiple of 4 stitches plus 2 in order for you to begin with 2 knit stitches and end neatly with another set of 2 knit stitches. In this case, if you cast on 84 stitches, you would not have the correct multiple; you would have to adjust your stitch count down to 82 or up to 86 in order to accommodate such a stitch pattern.

3 If you don't want your upsized sweater to fit snugly, add between 1″ and 6″ of ease to your bust measurement. This will give you the chest circumference of the sweater. Conversely, if you prefer a sweater with negative ease, subtract up to 3″. Divide this measurement by 2 (for the back and front), and multiply the resulting number by your stitch gauge for the number of stitches you need for the back (for instance, if your bust is 34″ and you've added 2″ of ease, then 34″ + 2″ = 36″; 36″ ÷ 2 = 18″; 18 x 6 stitches per inch = 108 stitches for the back after the armhole is complete). Subtract your crossback stitches (84) from the total number of stitches needed for the back (108), and divide this number by 2 for the number of stitches you need to add to each underarm (108 total back stitches – 84 crossback stitches = 24 total stitches to be added; 24 ÷ 2 = 12 stitches to be added to each underarm.

4 Cast on the number of stitches you calculated for your crossback for the back and follow the original pattern's stitch pattern or color patterning. Work the back without shaping until it almost reaches your underarm. This is where you will begin to shape the bottom of your armhole. Note that if you are working a sleeveless sweater, you may want to begin your armhole sooner, and work the armhole shaping more gradually, so that it covers the side of your bust better. The same is true if you have a large bust or are working a larger size, even if you plan on adding sleeves. Starting your armhole sooner will make the underarm fit better.

5 To shape the bottom of your armhole, just work a couple of increase rows (more if you began your armhole earlier) on each end of the right side of the piece and keep track of the number of stitches you need to add under each arm in total. Then, on your next right-side row, using a Backward Loop CO (see Special Techniques, page 152), cast on the remaining stitches for each underarm on each side of the garment. If your armhole

shaping is more gradual and worked over a longer distance, you might consider casting on the remaining stitches over several rows, rather than all at once. Work one wrong-side row, then carefully cut the yarn and place the back stitches on waste yarn.

Pay attention, however, to your stitch multiples when working in pattern. Remember in Step 2 you had a stitch pattern requiring a multiple of 4 stitches plus 2 to maintain the correct stitch multiple? Here is something to consider: If you are making a pullover, once you join it in the round, in order to keep your stitch pattern intact, you will need a multiple of 4 to maintain it. To remedy this, when you add your underarm stitches, keep track of the total number of body stitches you will end up having on your needles and adjust the total, if necessary.

6 Looking at what you have knit so far, which will look like a rectangle with a flared bottom where half of the underarm stitches are, determine how many stitches you will need for your back neck. If your or the recipient's back neck width is 5" and you want the neck opening to be wider than your neck, you might want a neck width of 6" (6" x 6 stitches per inch = 36 back neck stitches). *Note: Some designers automatically allocate one-third of the stitches to the back neck, so it is up to you if you want to do that.* Determine how many shoulder stitches you will have (84 crossback stitches – 36 neck stitches = 48 shoulder stitches for both shoulders ÷ 2 = 24 stitches for each shoulder). Carefully unravel the Provisional Cast-On and place the shoulder stitches (the first and last 24 stitches) back on your needle and the back neck stitches on waste yarn or a stitch holder. Attach a ball of yarn and work across the first shoulder/front. Drop your yarn, and attach another ball of yarn to the second shoulder/front and work to the end. Depending on how deep you want your neckline, work one or more inches of straight knitting without shaping so the fabric flows over the shoulders.

7 For a crewneck with a plain band or a turtleneck, on each right-side row, increase 1 stitch at each neck edge until you have added approximately a third of the required center neck stitches to each edge. (That is, 36 center neck stitches ÷ 3 = 12 stitches to be added to each side of the neck.) Then, using a Backward Loop CO, cast on the remaining neck stitches for the center front neck and join the front pieces together. You will have added 12 stitches to each side of the neck (24 stitches total), so you have a remainder of 12 stitches that you will need to cast on for the center neck. If you have a lot of stitches to add to each side, or a small number of rows over which to add the stitches, you may need to work a number of 2- or 3-stitch cast-ons in addition to or instead of 1-stitch increases, in order to add in all the stitches needed within the available number of rows. For a cardigan, never join in the round, just continue working the entire garment flat, with right-side and wrong-side rows.

8 Continue working as for the back, and work the increases for the underarm just as you did for the back. If necessary, try on the garment and decide if shaping is needed for the bustline, i.e., short rows (see page 18). On the next right-side row, you will join the pieces together, so place the back stitches that are currently on hold (the back stitches after working the armhole shaping, not the back neck stitches) onto a spare circular needle. On the next right-side row, work across the front, place a marker for the left side and beginning of the round, join the front to the back and work across the back, place a marker for the right side, and connect the back to the other side of the front. The garment is now all in one piece.

9 Work in the round or flat, adding waist shaping at the markers, if desired, and work down to the bottom edge. Read through the pattern or look at its schematic to see what kind of edging it has, plus its depth. Work your sweater similarly.

10 Read through the base pattern for sleeve instructions. Whether or not they are already top-down or bottom-up, a good way to work sleeves in this construction type is to add Afterthought Sleeves (see page 23). You'll just pick up stitches around the armholes and add the sleeves, altering stitch counts for a correct multiple of stitches, if necessary.

SIZES

XX-Small (X-Small, Small, Medium, Large, 1X-Large, 2X-Large, 3X-Large)

FINISHED MEASUREMENTS

32 (35, 37, 39, 42½, 45½, 48½, 51½)" chest

YARN

Cascade Greenland (100% merino superwash; 137 yards / 100 grams): 8 (9, 9, 9, 10, 11, 12, 12) balls #3537 Sapphire

NEEDLES

One 32" (80 cm) long or longer circular (circ) needle size US 9 (5.5 mm)

One or two 24" (60 cm) long circular needles or one set of five double-pointed needles (dpn) size US 9 (5.5 mm), as preferred, for Sleeves

Change needle size if necessary to obtain correct gauge.

NOTIONS

Stitch markers; waste yarn; one 16 (16, 16, 16, 18, 18, 18, 18)" long separating zipper; sewing needle and matching thread

GAUGE

16 sts and 21 rows = 4" (10 cm) in Stockinette stitch (St st)

HOLDEN JACKET

The Holden Jacket is a perfect unisex knit upon which you can base dozens of looks. It's easy to make simple alterations: add more texture by continuing the seed stitch the entire length of the sleeves; remove the seed stitch all together; or alter the neckline and collar as shown on page 58.

PATTERN FEATURES

Top-down raglan construction, incorporating simple stitch pattern into increases, short row shaping (described in the main version, optional), picking up and knitting.

STITCH PATTERN

Seed Stitch

(multiple of 2 sts; 1-row/rnd repeat)
Row/Rnd 1: *K1, p1; repeat from * to end.
Row/Rnd 2: Knit the purl sts and purl the knit sts as they face you.
Repeat Row/Rnd 2 for Seed Stitch.

YOKE

Using 32"-long circ needle, CO 2 sts for Left Front, pm, 6 (8, 8, 8, 6, 6, 4, 4) sts for Left Sleeve, pm, 24 (28, 28, 28, 30, 32, 34, 38) sts for Back, pm, 6 (8, 8, 8, 6, 6, 4, 4) sts for Right Sleeve, pm, and 2 sts for Right Front—40 (48, 48, 48, 46, 48, 46, 50) sts. Purl 1 row.

Note: Yoke and Neck shaping are worked at the same time; please read entire section through before beginning.

Shape Yoke

Increase Row 1 (RS): K1, [m1, k1, sm, k1, m1, work Seed st to 1 st before marker] 3 times, m1, k1, sm, k1, m1, k1—48 (56, 56, 56, 54, 56, 54, 58) sts. Work even for 1 row, working increased sts on Fronts in St st and on Back and Sleeves in Seed st, and working 1 st on either side of each marker in St st.

Increase Row 2 (RS): Increase 8 sts this row, then every other row 16 (17, 18, 18, 19, 20, 21, 22) times, as follows: Continuing to work st patterns as established, [work to 1 st before marker, m1, k1, sm, k1, m1] 4 times, work to end. AT THE SAME TIME, beginning on row 7 after CO, shape neck as follows.

Shape Neck (RS): Continuing with Yoke shaping as established, increase 1 st each neck edge this row, then every 4 rows 7 (7, 7, 7, 8, 7, 8, 8) times, as follows: K1, m1, work to last st, m1, k1. Work even for 1 row.

Next Row (RS): Using Backward Loop CO (see Special Techniques, page 152), CO 4 (4, 4, 4, 5, 5, 5, 5) sts, work to end, CO 4 (4, 4, 4, 5, 5, 5, 5) sts.

Next Row (RS): Work 4 (4, 4, 4, 5, 5, 5, 5) sts in Seed st, work to last 4 (4, 4, 4, 5, 5, 5, 5) sts, work in Seed st to end. Work even until Yoke shaping is complete, ending with a WS row—208 (224, 232, 232, 242, 250, 258, 270) sts.

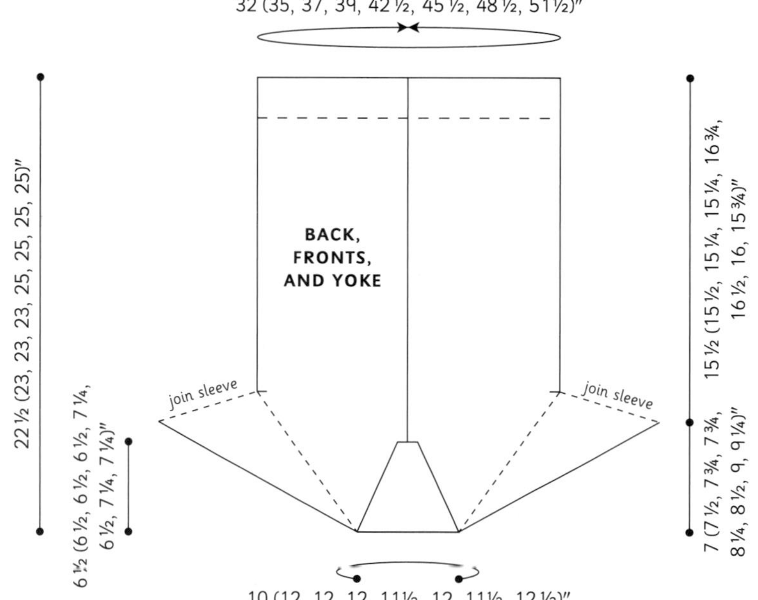

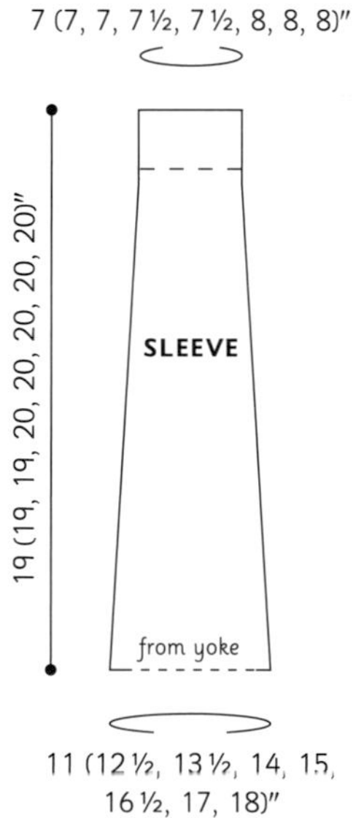

BODY

Next Row (RS): Knit across 32 (33, 34, 34, 37, 37, 39, 40) sts of left Front, transfer next 42 (46, 48, 48, 48, 50, 50, 52) sts to waste yarn for Left Sleeve, removing markers, CO 1 (2, 3, 5, 6, 8, 9, 10) st(s) for underarm, pm for side, CO 1 (2, 3, 5, 6, 8, 9, 10) st(s) for underarm, knit across 60 (66, 68, 68, 72, 76, 80, 86) sts of Back, transfer next 42 (46, 48, 48, 48, 50, 50, 52) sts to waste yarn for Right Sleeve, removing markers, CO 1 (2, 3, 5, 6, 8, 9, 10) st(s) for underarm, pm for side, CO 1 (2, 3, 5, 6, 8, 9, 10) st(s) for underarm, knit to end—128 (140, 148, 156, 170, 182, 194, 206) sts. Working back and forth, work even in patterns as established for 5 rows.

Shape Bust (optional)

Note: Bust will be shaped using Short Rows (see Special Techniques, page 156).

Row 1 (RS): Working back and forth on Left Front sts only, work to 5 sts before first marker, wrp-t.

Row 2: Work to end.

Row 3: Work to 4 sts before wrapped st of row before last row worked, wrp-t.

Row 4: Work to end.

Repeat Rows 3 and 4 once for a B cup, twice for a C cup, 3 times for a D cup, and so on, adding 1 more repeat of Rows 3 and 4 for each cup size over a D cup, and ending with a WS row.

Next Row (RS): Work across all sts, hiding all wraps as you come to them. Repeat for Right Front, working short rows on WS rows, and ending with a RS row.

Next Row (WS): Work across all sts, hiding all wraps as you come to them.

Next Row (RS): Work even in patterns as established until piece measures 13½ (13½, 13¼, 13¼, 14¾, 14½, 14, 13¾)" from underarm, ending with a WS row. Change to Seed st across all sts; work even for 2". BO all sts loosely in pattern.

SLEEVES

Note: Use your preferred method of working in the rnd when working the Sleeves (see page 23).

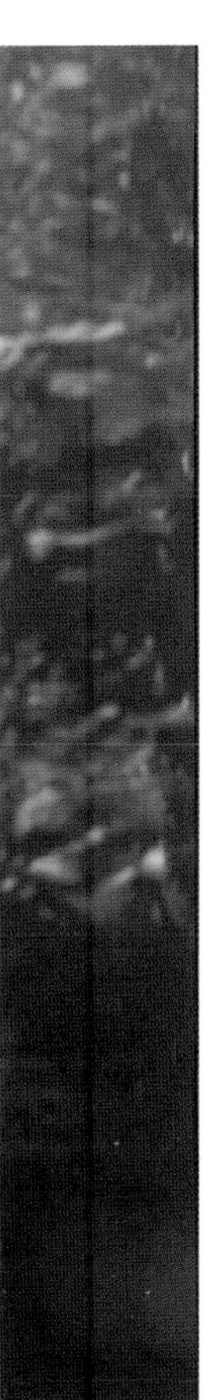

Transfer Sleeve sts from waste yarn to needle(s). With RS facing, join yarn at underarm; work to end, pick up and knit 1 (2, 3, 4, 6, 8, 9, 10) st(s) from st(s) CO for underarm, pm for beginning of rnd, pick up and knit 1 (2, 3, 4, 6, 8, 9, 10) st(s) from st(s) CO for underarm—44 (50, 54, 56, 60, 66, 68, 72) sts. Join for working in the rnd. Begin St st; work even for 5 rnds.

Shape Sleeve: Decrease 2 sts this rnd, every 11 (8, 7, 7, 6, 5, 5, 5) rnds 3 (3, 1, 6, 8, 14, 10, 2) time(s), then every 10 (7, 6, 6, 5, 4, 4, 4) rnds 4 (7, 11, 6, 6, 2, 7, 17) times, as follows: K1, k2tog, work to last 3 sts, ssk, k1—28 (28, 28, 30, 30, 32, 32, 32) sts remain. Work even until piece measures 17 (17, 17, 18, 18, 18, 18, 18)" from underarm, or to 2" from desired length. Change to Seed St; work even for 2". BO all sts loosely in pattern.

FINISHING

Collar: With RS facing, using 32"-long circ needle, beginning at Right Front neck edge, pick up and knit an even number of sts along Right Front neck shaping, across top of Right Sleeve, pm, across Back neck, pm, across Left Sleeve, then along Left Front neck shaping. Begin Seed st; work even for 1 row.

Shape Collar

Note: Collar is shaped using Short Rows. Hide wraps as you come to them.

Row 1 (RS): Work to second marker, wrp-t.

Row 2: Work to next marker, wrp-t.

Row 3: Work to wrapped st of row below last row worked, work wrapped st, work 2 sts, wrp-t.

Repeat Row 3 until you have reached the last st on each side. *Note: Depending on how many sts you picked up, you may have too few sts at the end of the row to wrap the last st.*

Work in Seed st across all sts for 9 rows, hiding remaining wrap as you come to it on first row. BO all sts in pattern.

Using sewing needle and matching thread, sew in zipper.

Block as desired.

MAKE IT YOUR OWN

Since this is a basic raglan, if you want to knit a size that isn't shown, just measure the back of the recipient's neck, multiply that number by your gauge, rounding up or down to get an even number, and cast on that number of stitches for the back neck and 2 or 3 stitches for each front and sleeve. Follow the stitch pattern and increases as written, but separate the body and sleeves when it "fits." See page 85 for tips on tweaking a top-down raglan for a custom fit. You can alter the neckline and add a polo collar, a Mandarin collar, or even a hood if you want. Work buttonhole and button bands for a button-up cardigan or shorten the sleeves.

The variation here was knit to fit a nine- to ten-year old boy, so I chose the smallest size—a 32" chest—thinking that a couple of inches of positive ease would be the way to go, both for room to grow and to allow him to run and play. I followed the pattern as is but omitted all body shaping. I raised the neckline by increasing the frequency of neckline shaping increments to every other row instead of every fourth row. Instead of the shawl collar shown in the main variation, this kid's variation has a simple polo collar which was made by picking up 4 stitches along the Seed stitch border and placing a marker. Then I picked up an even number of stitches along the back neck to the Seed stitch border and placed a marker, then 4 stitches along the top of the Seed stitch border. I kept the first and last set of 4 stitches in Seed stitch and worked 2x2 ribbing for 5" before binding off. The zipper was added last.

The variation was worked in the smallest size with 6 balls of Cascade Greenland in color #3539. Read about estimating yarn requirements on page 15.

SIZES

XXX-Small (XX-Small, Small, Medium, Large, 1X-Large, 2X-Large, 3X-Large)

FINISHED MEASUREMENTS

30 (32, 34, 36, 40, 44, 48, 50)" chest

YARN

Lana Grossa Royal Tweed (100% fine merino; 110 yards / 50 grams): 7 (8, 8, 9, 9, 11, 11, 11) balls #021 Red

NEEDLES

One 32" (80 cm) long or longer circular (circ) needle size US 8 (5 mm)

One or two 24" (60 cm) long or longer circular needles or one set of five double-pointed needles (dpn) size US 8 (5 mm), as preferred, for Sleeves

Change needle size if necessary to obtain correct gauge.

NOTIONS

Waste yarn; removable stitch marker; stitch markers in 3 colors

GAUGE

16 sts and 24 rows = 4" (10 cm) in Stockinette stitch (St st)

PEBBLES

This sweater is literally worked "inside out" to expose the seams and show off the purl stitches that normally hide on the inside. It's a classic look with a bit more edge. Of course, if you decide to skip the "edge," you can always weave in your ends accordingly and wear it with the knit side out.

PATTERN FEATURES

Top-down set-in-sleeve construction, provisional cast-on, simple shaping, ribbing, picking up and knitting, short-row shaping.

STITCH PATTERN

2x2 Rib

(multiple of 4 sts; 1-rnd repeat)

All Rnds: *K2, p2; repeat from * to end.

NOTE

The Reverse Stockinette stitch (purl) side of this sweater is the RS. To make knitting the sweater easier, it is worked inside out, so that you work with the knit side facing you. Before you join the Body, you will work in Stockinette stitch, with the knit rows as RS rows and the purl rows as WS rows. Once you join the body, you will continue to work in Stockinette stitch, knitting all rounds. Once the sweater is complete, you will turn the sweater inside out so that the knit side is now the WS and the purl side is the RS. If you are working the piece as written, remember that the yarn tail should be to the knit side when you join a new ball of yarn, so that it won't show once the sweater is turned inside out.

BACK

Note: After the initial Provisional CO, use Backward Loop CO for any other COs in this pattern (see Special Techniques, page 152). You will be working with the knit side as the RS, but it will become the WS when the piece is finished; remember to keep yarn tails to the knit side when joining a new ball of yarn. Using longer circ needle, waste yarn and Provisional CO, CO 50 (52, 54, 56, 60, 64, 68, 72) sts. Change to working yarn; begin St st. Work even until piece measures 6 (6 ½, 6 ¾, 7, 7 ¼, 6 ¾, 7 ¼, 7 ¼)" from the beginning, ending with a WS row.

Shape Armholes (RS): Increase 1 st each side this row, then every other row 0 (0, 0, 0, 0, 1, 1, 1) time(s), as follows: K1, m1, knit to last st, m1, k1—52 (54, 56, 58, 62, 68, 72, 76) sts. Work even for 1 row.

Next Row (RS): CO 2 (2, 3, 3, 2, 3, 3, 3) sts at beginning of next 2 rows, 2 (3, 3, 4, 3, 3, 4, 4) sts at beginning of next 2 rows, then 0 (0, 0, 0, 4, 4, 5, 5) sts at beginning of next 2 rows—60 (64, 68, 72, 80, 88, 96, 100) sts. Transfer sts to waste yarn for Body. Break yarn.

FRONT

With RS facing, carefully unravel Provisional CO and place sts on circ needle. (RS) K18 (18, 19, 20, 21, 22, 24, 24) sts for right Front, join a second ball of yarn, BO center 14 (16, 16, 16, 18, 20, 20, 24) sts, purl to end for left Front. Place removable marker for top of shoulder. Working BOTH SIDES AT SAME TIME using separate balls of yarn, begin St st, beginning with a purl row; work even for 15 rows.

Shape Neck (RS): Increase 1 st each neck edge this row, then every other row 2 (3, 3, 3, 4, 4, 4, 4) times, as follows: On right Front, work to last st, m1, k1; on left Front, k1, m1, work to end—21 (22, 23, 24, 26, 27, 29, 29) sts each side. Work even for 1 row.

Join Fronts (RS): Work to end of right Front, CO 0 (0, 0, 0, 0, 1, 1, 3) sts, pm for center panel, CO 8 sts for center panel, pm, CO 0 (0, 0, 0, 0, 1, 1, 3) sts, work across left Front—50 (52, 54, 56, 60, 64, 68, 72) sts.

Next Row (WS): Purl to first center panel marker, [k2, p1] twice, k2, purl to end. Work even, knitting the knit sts and purling the purl sts as they face you, until piece measures same as for Back from top of shoulder to beginning of armhole shaping, ending with a WS row. Shape armholes as for Back—60 (64, 68, 72, 80, 88, 96, 100) sts.

BODY

Join Back and Front (RS): Work across Front sts, keeping center panel in ribbing as established, pm for side, work across Back sts from waste yarn—120 (128, 136, 144, 160, 176, 192, 200) sts. Join for working in the rnd; pm for side and beginning of rnd. Work even until piece measures 5 (5, 5 ¼, 5 ½, 5 ¼, 5 ¾, 5 ¾, 5 ¾)" from underarm.

Shape Waist: Decrease 4 sts this rnd, then every 6 rnds twice, as follows: [K1, k2tog, work to 3 sts before side marker, ssk, k1, sm] twice—108 (116, 124, 132, 148, 164, 180, 188) sts remain. Work even for 5 rnds.

Shape Hip: Increase 4 sts this rnd, then every 6 rnds twice, as follows: [K1, m1, work to 1 st before side marker, m1, k1, sm] twice—120 (128, 136, 144, 160, 176, 192, 200) sts. Work even until piece measures 12 (11½, 11¼, 11, 10 ½, 11½, 11, 11)", or to 3" from

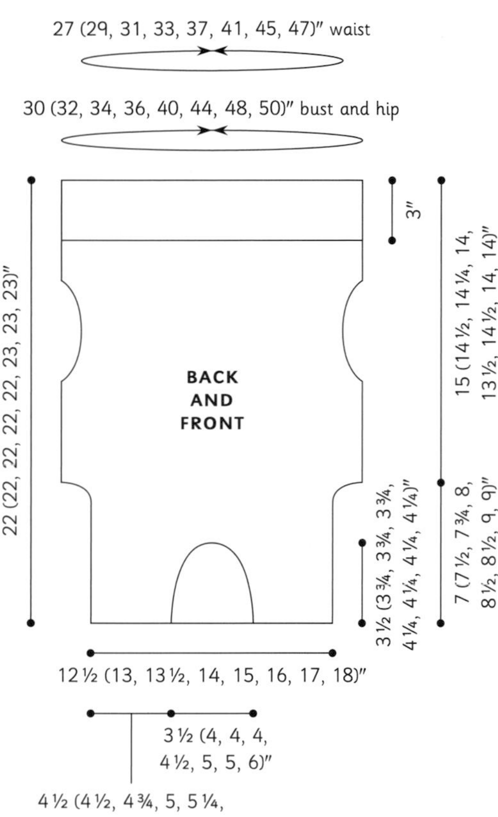

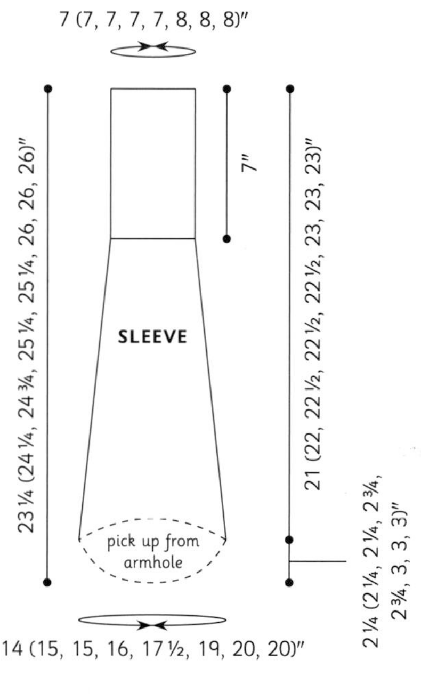

desired length from underarm, decrease 2 sts evenly spaced on last rnd, working decreases outside center ribbed panel—118 (126, 134, 142, 158, 174, 190, 198) sts.

Next Rnd: Knit to first center panel marker, work 8 sts as established, *k2, p2; repeat from * through beginning of rnd to 2 sts before first center panel marker, k2, work in ribbing as established to beginning of rnd. Work even for 3". BO all sts loosely in pattern.

SLEEVES

Note: Use your preferred method of working in the rnd when working the Sleeves (see page 23). You will be using 5 markers in 3 different colors: 1 color for beginning of rnd, 2 of color A to mark end of cap shaping, and 2 of color B to mark center of cap shaping.

Turn Body inside out so that purl side is facing; the purl side is now the RS. Beginning at bottom center of underarm, pick up and knit 56 (60, 60, 64, 70, 76, 80, 80) sts as follows: 6 (7, 7, 7, 8, 9, 10, 10) sts, pm color A, 13 (13, 13, 15, 15, 17, 17, 17) sts, pm color B, 18 (20, 20, 20, 24, 24, 26, 26) sts, pm color B, 13 (13, 13, 15, 15, 17, 17, 17) sts, pm color A, 6 (7, 7, 7, 8, 9, 10, 10) sts. *Note: Be sure to pick up the same number of sts between bottom center of armhole and top of shoulder on both sides of the armhole. Color B markers should be equidistant from top of shoulder. If you would prefer not to place markers while you pick up sts, you may first pick up the total number of sts required, join for working in the rnd, then knit 1 rnd, placing the markers according to the numbers given in the pick-up instructions.* Slip 1 st, wrp-t; knit side (WS) is now facing.

Shape Cap

Note: Cap will be shaped using Short Rows (see Special Techniques, page 156). Hide wraps as you come to them. You will be working with the knit side as the RS, but it will become the WS when the piece is finished; remember to keep yarn tails to the knit side when joining a new ball of yarn.

Row 1: Working back and forth, begin St st, beginning with a knit row. Work to second color B marker, sm, wrp-t.

Row 2: Repeat Row 1.

Row 3: Work to wrapped st of row before last row worked, work wrapped st, work 1 st, wrp-t.

Repeat Row 3 until you have reached the color A markers on each side of Sleeve.

Next Rnd (WS): Change to working in the rnd, hiding remaining wraps as you come to them, and removing all markers; pm for beginning of rnd. Work even for 4 (4, 4, 4, 3, 3, 3, 3) rnds.

Shape Sleeve: Decrease 2 sts this rnd, every 6 (6, 6, 5, 4, 4, 4, 4) rnds 5 (1, 4, 11, 20, 20, 14, 14) time(s), then every 5 (5, 5, 4, 0, 3, 3, 3) rnds 8 (14, 11, 6, 0, 1, 9, 9) time(s), as follows: K1, k2tog, work to last 3 sts, ssk, k1—28 (28, 28, 28, 28, 32, 32, 32) sts. Work even until piece measures 14 (15, 15½, 15½, 15½, 16, 16, 16)", measuring from bottom center of underarm, or to 7" from desired length.

Change to 2x2 Rib; work even for 7". BO all sts loosely in pattern.

FINISHING

Neckband: With RS (purl side) facing, using shorter circ needle and beginning at center Back neck, pick up and knit a multiple of 4 sts to 8 center Front ribbed sts, pm, pick up and knit 1 st in each of 8 center Front ribbed sts, pm, pick up and knit a multiple of 4 sts plus 2 to center Back neck. Join for working in the rnd; pm for beginning of rnd.

Next Rnd: *K2, p2; repeat from * to first marker, sm, [k2, p1] twice, k2, sm, *p2, k2; repeat from * to last 2 sts, p2. Work even for 3 rnds. BO all sts loosely in pattern.

Block as desired.

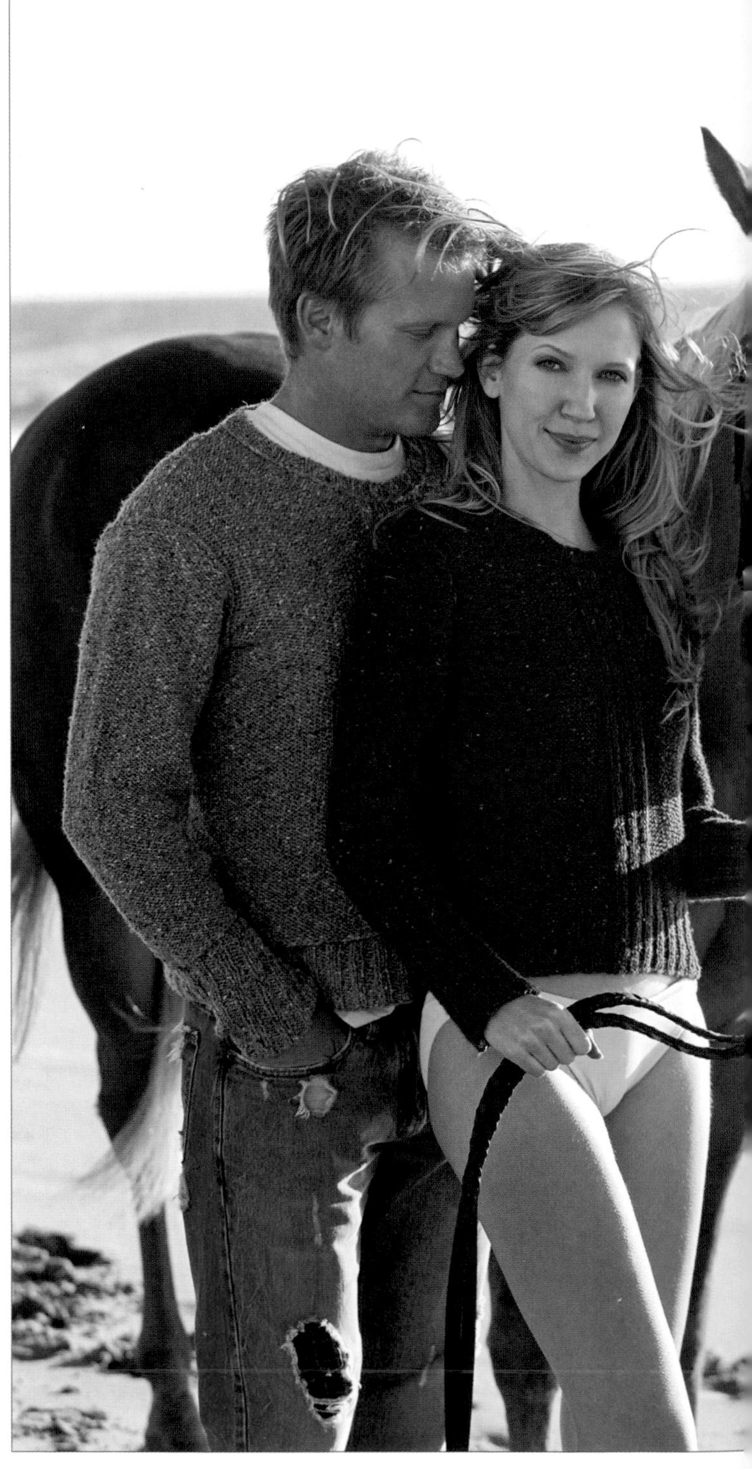

MAKE IT YOUR OWN

Play around a bit and decide for yourself how deconstructed you want your own sweater to look. Want exposed seams where you pick up stitches (as for the men's sweater)? Just make sure the wrong side is facing when you pick them up. If you'd rather have a Stockinette stitch sweater, knit it in the round with the public (right) side facing you.

Since this pattern is sized to a 50" chest, converting it to fit a man is easy—though you'll still need to figure out the measurements for his armhole depth and body and sleeve lengths. See page 48 for a chart that gives men's sizing. If you compare the measurements, particularly the crossback and sleeve length to the schematics in the base pattern presented here, creating the men's version is a breeze. The men's version shown here was based on the woman's 40" bust size, with a few changes to make it more masculine. When casting stitches on for the back, begin with a conventional cast-on rather than a provisional cast-on. When it's time to work the Front, pick up stitches from the Back's cast-on stitches with the knit side facing. This will create a seam that will be visible on the purl side when the sweater is turned inside out. It will also have the added benefit of giving more stability to larger sized or heavier garments.

Work one extra inch before beginning the armhole shaping for both Back and Front as given in the pattern. Then work the Body, omitting the waist and hip shaping, until the piece is 3" from the desired total length. Bind off all the stitches. With the knit side facing, pick up stitches around the bound-off edge, beginning after the center panel, and ending before it, making sure you have a multiple of 4 stitches plus 2; place a marker before the center panel, pick up 1 stitch in each of the 8 center panel stitches, place a marker after the center panel. Work the ribbing as follows: K2, *p2, k2; repeat from * to first center panel marker, [p2, k1] twice, p2. Continue knitting the knit stitches and purling the purl stitches until piece measures 3" from the pick-up round. Bind off all stitches in pattern.

When working the Sleeves, follow the women's pattern, but you will need to pick up more stitches around the armholes due to their increased depth. On page 23, you'll find a section on Afterthought Sleeves that will help you decide how to calculate the number of stitches that should be allocated for the sleeve cap shaping. After shaping the sleeve cap, and before knitting down to where you bind off, you may decide to increase the number of rounds between decrease rounds so that you complete the decreases close to the end of the Sleeve.

In order to create a visible seam on this variation, before you begin the ribbing, bind off all stitches instead. Then with the knit side facing, pick up and knit a multiple of 4 stitches around the bound-off edge. Work 2x2 Rib for 7" and bind off all stitches in pattern.

This variation was worked in size 40, with 7 balls of GGH Silky Tweed in color 7. Read about estimating yarn requirements on page 15.

FLANNEL JACKET

This jacket is high in style and quick and fun to make. It is a little heavier than average because the yarn is bulky, so you may want to stabilize the shoulders. If you do, go ahead and skip the provisional cast-on, working a regular cast-on instead, and when it's time to work the Fronts, pick up and knit the required number of shoulder stitches. That way, you'll have a line of stitches on the inside of the shoulder that will act as a "seam." Other ideas for stabilizing shoulders in seamless garments can be found on page 25.

PATTERN FEATURES

Top-down set-in-sleeve construction, provisional cast-on, simple stitch pattern, picking up and knitting, short-row shaping.

SIZES

4 (6, 8, 10) <XX-Small (X-Small, Small, Medium, Large, 1X-Large, 2X-Large, 3X-Large)>

Instructions for girls' sizes are given first; women's sizes are between < >. If only one number is given, it applies to both sizes.

FINISHED MEASUREMENTS

26½ (28¼, 29¾, 31½) <35 (38¼, 41¾, 45, 48½, 51¾, 55¼, 58½)>" chest, including bands, overlapped

YARN

Girls': Brown Sheep Co. Lamb's Pride Bulky (85% wool / 15% mohair; 125 yards / 113 grams): 3 (4, 4, 5) skeins #M-162 Mulberry or #M-120 Limeade

Women's: Spud & Chloë Outer (65% superwash wool / 35% organic cotton; 60 yards / 100 grams): 7 (8, 8, 10, 11, 11, 11, 12) hanks #7201 Flannel

NEEDLES

One 32" (80 cm) long or longer circular needle size US 11 (8 mm)

One or two 24" (60 cm) long or longer circular needles or one set of five double-pointed needles (dpn) size US 11 (8 mm), as preferred, for Sleeves

Change needle size if necessary to obtain correct gauge.

NOTIONS

Waste yarn; removable marker; stitch markers in 3 colors; 1¼ <1½> yards 2" wide ribbon; sewing needle and thread; 10 mm <30 mm> sew-on snap

GAUGE

9½ sts and 20 rows = 4" (10 cm) in Stockinette stitch (St st)

STITCH PATTERNS

Seeded Rib (worked flat)

(multiple of 4 sts + 3; 2-row repeat)

Row 1 (WS): K1, *p1, k3; repeat from *last 2 sts, p1, k1.

Row 2: K3, *p1, k3; repeat from * to end.

Repeat Rows 1 and 2 for Seeded Rib (worked flat).

Seeded Rib (worked in the rnd)

(multiple of 4 sts; 2-rnd repeat)

Rnd 1: *K2, p1, k1; repeat from * to end.

Rnd 2: *K1, p3; repeat from * to end.

Repeat Rnds 1 and 2 for Seeded Rib (worked in the rnd).

BACK

Note: After the initial Provisional CO, use Backward Loop CO for any other COs in this pattern (see Special Techniques, page 152).

Using 32"-long circ needle, waste yarn and Provisional CO, CO 22 (24, 26, 28) <30 (34, 34, 38, 40, 42, 42, 42)> sts. (RS) Change to working yarn; begin St st. Work even until piece measures 3¾ (4¼, 4¼, 4¾) <6¼ (6½, 6¼, 7, 7, 7½, 7½, 8)>" from the beginning, ending with a WS row.

Shape Armholes (RS): Increase 1 st each side this row, then every other row 2 <1 (1, 2, 1, 2, 2, 2, 2)> time(s), as follows: K1, m1, work to last st, m1, k1—28 (30, 32, 34) <34 (38, 40, 42, 46, 48, 48, 48)> sts. Work even for 1 row.

Next Row (RS): CO 0 <2 (2, 3, 2, 2, 3, 4, 4)> st(s) at beginning of next 2 rows, then 0 <0 (0, 0, 2, 2, 2, 3, 5)> st(s) at beginning of next 2 rows—28 (30, 32, 34) <38 (42, 46, 50, 54, 58, 62, 66)> sts. Transfer sts to waste yarn for Body.

FRONT

With RS facing, carefully unravel Provisional CO and place sts on longer circ needle. K6 (6, 7, 7) <9 (11, 11, 12, 13, 14, 14, 14)>, join a second ball of yarn, BO center 10 (12, 12, 14) <12 (12, 12, 14, 14, 14, 14, 14)> sts, knit to end. Place removable marker for top of shoulder. Working BOTH SIDES AT SAME TIME using separate balls of yarn, begin St st, beginning with a purl row; work even for 5 (5, 7, 7) <7> rows.

Shape Neck (RS): Increase 1 st each neck edge this row, then every other row 2 (3, 3, 4) <3 (3, 3, 4, 4, 4, 4, 4)> times, as follows: On Right Front, knit to last st, m1, k1; on Left Front, k1, m1, knit to end—9 (10, 11, 12) <13 (15, 15, 17, 18, 19, 19, 19)> sts. Work even for 1 row.

Next Row (RS): On Right Front, work to end, CO 2 sts; on Left Front, CO 2 sts, work to end—11 (12, 13, 14) <15 (17, 17, 19, 20, 21, 21, 21)> sts. Work even until piece measures same as for Back from top of shoulder to beginning of armhole shaping. Shape armholes as for Back, ending with a WS row—14 (15, 16, 17) <19 (21, 23, 25, 27, 29, 31, 33)> sts each Front. Break yarn for Right Front.

BODY

Join Back and Fronts (RS): With RS facing, transfer Back sts, then Right Front sts to left-hand end of circ needle. Your sts should now be in the following order, from right to left, with RS facing: Left Front, Back, Right Front. Using yarn attached to Left Front, knit across Left Front, k1 from Back, m1, knit across Back, then Right Front—57 (61, 65, 69) <77 (85, 93, 101, 109, 117, 125, 133)> sts. Working in St st, work even until piece measures 7 (7½, 9, 9½) <8½ (9¼, 9¼, 10½, 11, 10½, 10½, 10)>" or to 2½" from desired length from underarm, ending with a WS row. Change to Seeded Rib (worked flat); work even for 2½". BO all sts loosely knitwise.

SLEEVES

Note: Use your preferred method of working in the rnd when working the Sleeves (see page 23). You will be using 3 different color markers; one color for beginning of rnd, 2 of color A to mark end of cap shaping, and 2 of color B to mark center of cap shaping.

With RS facing, beginning at bottom center of underarm, pick up and knit 28 (32, 32, 36) <36 (40, 40, 44, 48, 50, 50, 54) > sts as follows: 3 (4, 4, 5) <4 (5, 5, 6, 6, 6, 6, 7)> sts, pm color A, 7 <9 (9, 9, 9, 10, 11, 11, 11)> sts, pm color B, 8 (10, 10, 12) <10 (12, 12, 14, 16, 16, 16, 18)> sts, pm color B, 7 <9 (9, 9, 9, 10, 11, 11, 11)> sts, pm color A, 3 (4, 4, 5) <4 (5, 5, 6, 6, 6, 6, 7)> sts. *Note: Be sure to pick up the same number of sts between bottom center of armhole and top of shoulder*

on both sides of the armhole. Color B markers should be equidistant from top of shoulder. If you would prefer not to place markers while you pick up sts, you may first pick up the total number of sts required, join for working in the rnd, then knit 1 rnd, placing the markers according to the numbers given in the pick-up instructions.

Shape Cap

Note: Cap will be shaped using Short Rows (see Special Techniques, page 156). Hide wraps as you come to them.

Row 1 (RS): Working back and forth, begin St st, work to second color B marker, sm, wrp-t.

Row 2: Repeat Row 1.

Row 3: Work to wrapped st of row below last row worked, work wrapped st, work 1 st, wrp-t.

Repeat Row 3 until you have reached the color A markers on each side of the Sleeve.

Next Row (RS): Change to working in the rnd, hiding remaining wrap as you come to it and removing all markers except beginning of rnd marker. Work even for 0 <4 (4, 4, 2, 2, 2, 2, 2)> rnds.

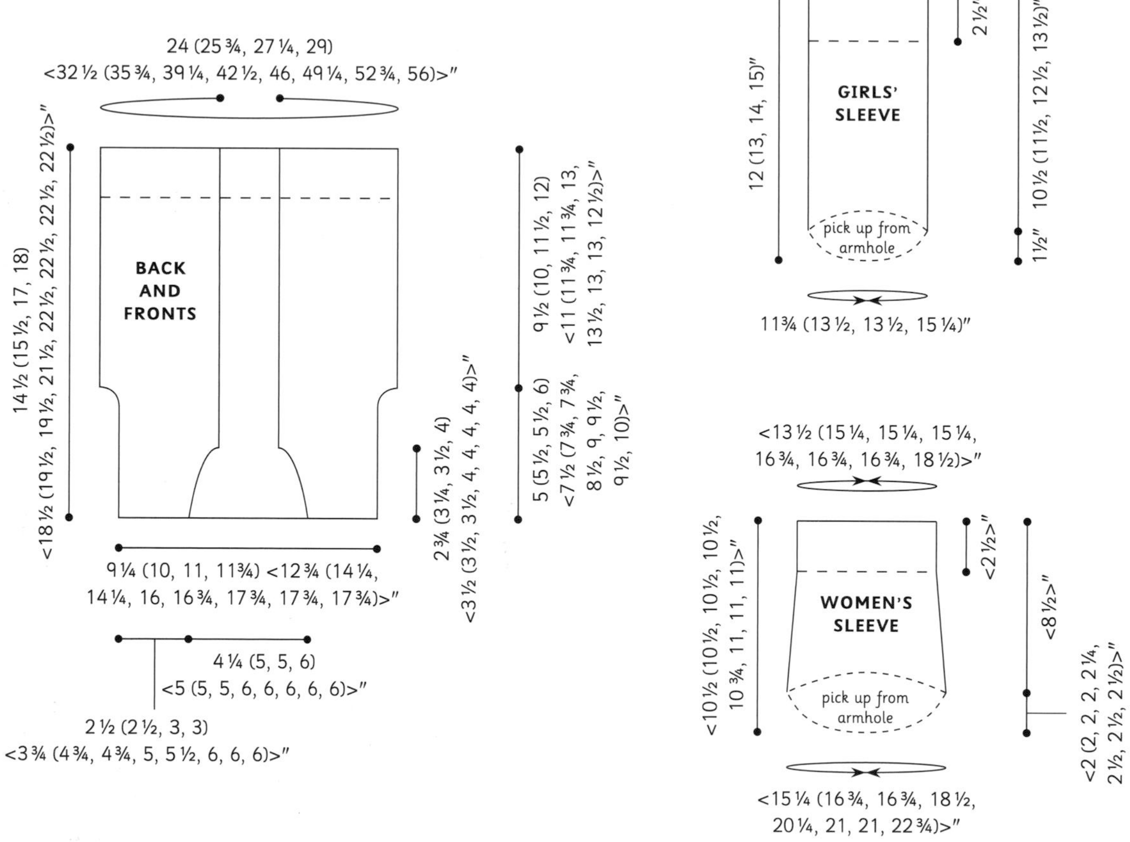

Women's Sizes Only:

Shape Sleeve: Decrease 2 sts this rnd, then every 6 (6, 6, 4, 4, 4, 4, 4) rnds 1 (1, 1, 3, 3, 4, 4, 4) time(s), as follows: K1, k2tog, work to last 3 sts, ssk, k1—32 (36, 36, 36, 40, 40, 40, 44) sts remain.

All Sizes:

Next Rnd: Work even until piece measures 8 (9, 10, 11) <6>", measuring from bottom center of underarm, or to 2 ½" from desired length. Change to Seeded Rib (worked in the rnd); work even for 2 ½". BO all sts loosely knitwise.

FINISHING

Collar: With RS facing, using shorter circ needle, beginning at Right Front neck edge, pick up and knit a multiple of 4 sts + 3 around neck opening. Begin Seeded Rib (worked flat); work even until piece measures 4 (4 ½, 4 ½, 5) <5>" from pick-up row, ending with a WS row. BO all sts loosely knitwise.

Front Bands: With RS facing, using shorter circ needle, beginning at bottom Right Front edge, pick up and knit a multiple of 4 sts + 3 along Right Front edge, ending at top edge of Collar. Begin Seeded Rib (worked flat); work even until piece measures 2 ½" from pick-up row, ending with a WS row. BO all sts loosely knitwise. Repeat for Left Front, beginning at top edge of Collar.

Cut 2 lengths of ribbon long enough to fit Front Bands and Collar, plus ¼" at each end for finishing. Using sewing thread, sew ribbon to RS of Left Front Band, folding ¼" of ribbon under at each end for a neat edge. Repeat for Right Front Band, sewing ribbon to WS of Band. Sew on snap at base of Collar; sew snap a little higher on one side for an asymmetrical look (optional).

Block as desired.

MAKE IT YOUR OWN

This jacket lends itself to a variety of looks, plus it's a cinch to customize. Experiment with the placement of the snap so it appears asymmetrical or perfectly balanced. Add length to the sleeves and body for a car-coat look. Or downsize for a little girl—or two—in similar bulky yarn. The kid-sized versions are included in the instructions, before the brackets, or take a look at the section on downsizing a pattern on page 50 to custom-make a miniature version to your own specifications.

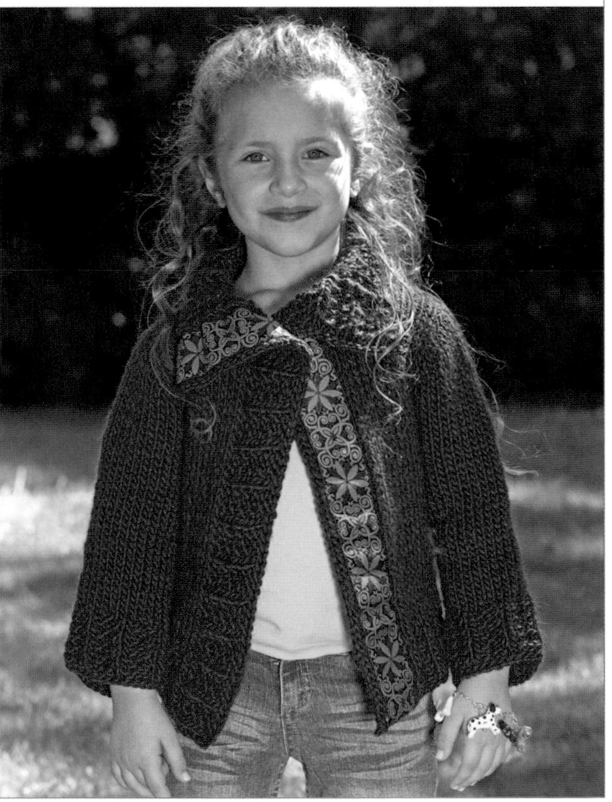

SIZES

XX-Small (X-Small, Small, Medium, Large, 1X-Large, 2X-Large, 3X-Large)

FINISHED MEASUREMENTS

30 (32¾, 34¾, 36¾, 40¾, 45¼, 48, 54)" chest

YARN

Blue Sky Alpacas Sport Weight (100% baby alpaca; 110 yards / 50 grams): 5 (6, 6, 7, 7, 8, 9, 10) hanks #535 Bluejay

NEEDLES

One 29" (70 cm) long or longer circular (circ) needle size US 5 (3.75 mm)

One 29" (70 cm) long circular needle size US 3 (3.25 mm)

One 16" (40 cm) long circular needle size US 3 (3.25 mm)

Change needle size if necessary to obtain correct gauge.

NOTIONS

Waste yarn; removable markers; stitch markers; cable needle (cn)

GAUGE

24 sts and 30 rows = 4" (10 cm) in Stockinette stitch (St st), using larger needles

STAGHORN VEST

This top-down vest is perfect on its own or as a layering piece, adding just the right amount of style and warmth nearly any time of year. But best of all, it is the ultimate in customizable garments. Although the main pattern is written for a woman, the cables are so classic and gender-neutral they can be worn by a woman or a man, or omitted altogether. (see the variation on page 76).

PATTERN FEATURES

Top-down construction, provisional cast-on, simple shaping, cables, picking up and knitting, ribbing.

ABBREVIATIONS

BC: Slip next 2 sts to cn, hold to back, k2, k2 from cn.

FC: Slip next 2 sts to cn, hold to front, k2, k2 from cn.

STITCH PATTERNS

Reverse Staghorn Cable

(panel of 20 sts; 6-rnd repeat)
Rnds 1, 3, and 5: P2, k16, p2.
Rnd 2: P2, FC, k8, BC, p2.
Rnd 4: P2, k2, FC, k4, BC, k2, p2.
Rnd 6: P2, k4, FC, BC, k4, p2.
Repeat Rnds 1–6 for Reverse Staghorn Cable.

1x1 Rib

(multiple of 2 sts; 1-rnd repeat)
All Rnds: *K1, p1; repeat from * to end.

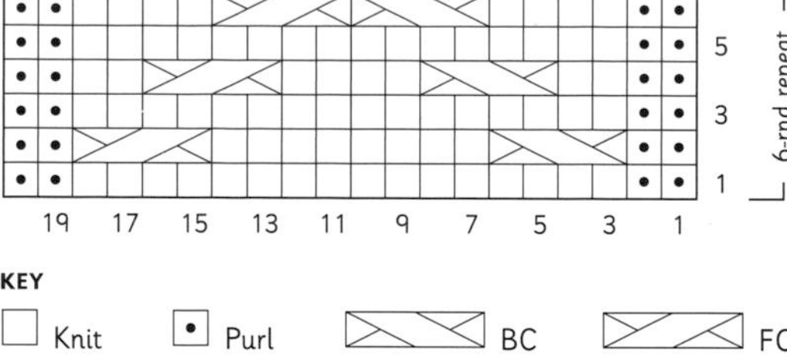

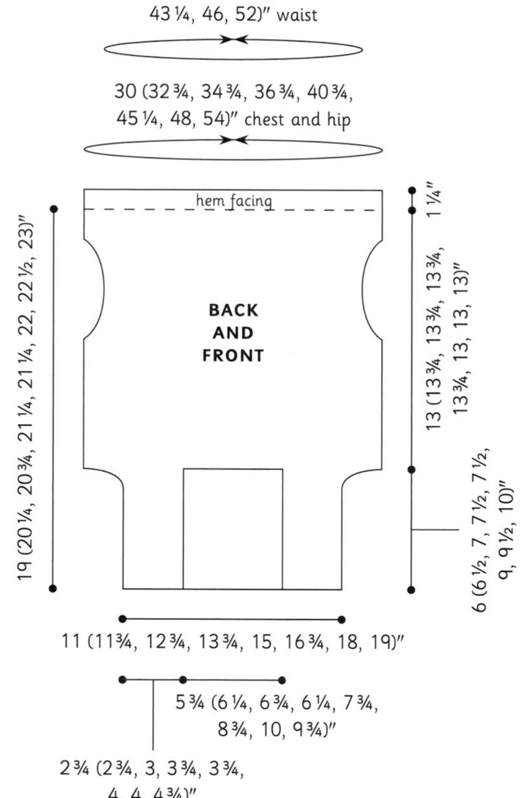

BACK

Note: After the initial Provisional CO, use Backward Loop CO for any other COs in this pattern (see Special Techniques, page 152). Using larger circ needle, waste yarn and Provisional CO, CO 66 (70, 76, 82, 90, 100, 108, 114) sts. (RS) Change to working yarn, begin St st. Work even until piece measures 4¾ (5¼, 5¾, 6¼, 6, 6¾, 7¼, 7¾)" from the beginning, ending with a WS row.

Shape Armholes (RS): Increase 1 st each side this row, then every other row 1 (1, 1, 1, 1, 3, 3, 3) time(s), as follows: K1, m1, knit to last st, m1, k1—70 (74, 80, 86, 94, 108, 116, 122) sts. Work even for 1 row.

Next Row (RS): CO 2 (2, 2, 2, 2, 3, 3, 3) sts at beginning of next 2 rows, 3 (4, 4, 4, 3, 3, 3, 5) sts at beginning of next 2 rows, 5 (6, 6, 6, 4, 4, 4, 6) sts at beginning of next 2 rows, then 0 (0, 0, 0, 5, 4, 4, 6) sts at beginning of next 2 rows—90 (98, 104, 110, 122, 136, 144, 162) sts. Transfer sts to waste yarn for Body. Break yarn.

FRONT

With RS facing, carefully unravel Provisional CO and place sts on larger circ needle. (RS) K16 (16, 18, 22, 22, 24, 24, 28), join a second ball of yarn, BO center 34 (38, 40, 38, 46, 52, 60, 58) sts, knit to end. Place removable marker for top of shoulder. Working BOTH SIDES AT SAME TIME using separate balls of yarn, continue in St st until piece measures same as for Back from top of shoulder to beginning of armhole shaping, ending with a WS row. Shape armholes as for Back—28 (30, 32, 36, 38, 42, 42, 52) sts each side. Break yarn for left Front.

BODY

Join Back and Front (RS): Knit across right Front sts, CO 3 (5, 6, 5, 5, 4, 8, 7) sts, pm, CO 4 (4, 4, 4, 8, 12, 12, 12) sts, pm, CO 20 sts, pm, CO 4 (4, 4, 4, 8, 12, 12, 12) sts, pm, CO 3 (5, 6, 5, 5, 4, 8, 7) sts, knit across left Front sts, pm for side, knit across Back sts from waste yarn—180 (196, 208, 220, 244, 272, 288, 324) sts. Join for working in the rnd; pm for beginning of rnd.

Set-Up Rnd: Work to first marker, sm, [p2, k2] 1 (1, 1, 1, 2, 3, 3, 3) time(s), sm, work Rnd 1 of Reverse Staghorn Cable, sm, [k2, p2] 1 (1, 1, 1, 2, 3, 3, 3) time(s), sm, knit to end.

Next Rnd: Knitting the knit sts and purling the purl sts as they face you, work to second marker, sm, work Rnd 1 of Reverse Staghorn Cable again, sm, work to end. Work even in patterns as established (working Rnd 2 of Reverse Staghorn Cable on first rnd) until piece measures 6 ¾ (6 ¼, 6 ¼, 6 ¼, 6, 4 ¾, 4 ¼, 4 ¼)" from underarm.

Shape Waist: Decrease 4 sts this rnd, then every 7 rnds twice, as follows: [K1, k2tog, work to 3 sts before side marker, ssk, k1, sm] twice—168 (184, 196, 208, 232, 260, 276, 312) sts remain. Work even for 7 rnds.

Shape Hip: Increase 4 sts this rnd, then every 7 rnds twice, as follows: [K1, m1, work to 1 st before side marker, m1, k1, sm] twice—180 (196, 208, 220, 244, 272, 288, 324) sts. Work even until piece measures approximately 13 (13 ¾, 13 ¾, 13 ¾, 13 ¾, 13, 13, 13)" from underarm, ending with Rnd 1 of Reverse Staghorn Cable. Purl 1 rnd (turning rnd). Change to smaller 29" long circ needle and St st; work even for 9 rnds. BO all sts loosely.

FINISHING

Fold hem to WS at turning rnd and sew to WS, being careful not to let sts show on RS.

Neckband: Using removable markers, mark bottom corner sts of Front neck opening. With RS facing, using smaller 16" circ needle, beginning at right edge of Back neck, pick up and knit 1 st for every CO st across Back neck, approximately 3 sts for every 4 rows down left Front to first marked st, making sure to pick up an even number of sts, pm, 1 st for every CO st across Front neck to second marked st, pm, and approximately 3 sts for every 4 rows up right Front to shoulder, making sure to end with an even number of sts.

Rnd 1: Begin 1x1 Rib; work to 2 sts before first neck marker, skp, work in rib, beginning with a knit st, to second neck marker, k2tog, work in rib, beginning with a knit st, to end. Repeat Rnd 1 three times, working rib pattern as established. BO all sts loosely in pattern.

Armhole Edging: With RS facing, using 16" circ needle, and beginning at center underarm, pick up and knit approximately 3 sts for every 4 sts or rows around armhole, making sure to end with an even number of sts. Begin 1x1 Rib; work even for 4 rnds. BO all sts loosely in pattern.

Block as desired.

MAKE IT YOUR OWN

If you'd like to make this vest less complicated, simply strip away the shaping and the cable motif. This pattern can also be converted to a simple men's version like the one shown here. Instead of a square neck, make a V-neck for a classic men's style, and add ribbing at the bottom instead of the hem as shown on the woman's version. You can swap out the center panel cable motif with a motif of your choosing, but if you're using a stitch pattern book, make sure you like the cable when it's turned upside down—since you'll be working the sweater top-down, the cable is essentially worked upside down. Adding sleeves of any kind to this sort of top-down construction is a snap (see Afterthought Sleeves on page 23.)

To make the men's version, check that the pattern has a similar crossback and chest measurement that will fit the person for whom it is intended. Make note of the required armhole depth (men's tend to be an inch or two deeper than women's—see page 48 for sample men's measurements and more detail about converting a women's pattern into a men's), and cast on. Follow the instructions for the Back and begin shaping the armholes an inch or two later than written in the pattern (or whatever depth is necessary to match the recipient's measurements) to accommodate deeper armholes. To make the V-neck, after placing the shoulder stitches on the needles, work the two Fronts even for 1". After that, begin increasing 1 stitch on each neck edge every right side row until the sum of the two Fronts equals the number of stitches that were initially cast on for the Back. On the next right-side row, join the two Front sides and continue working the Front, shaping the underarms as for the Back. Join in the round, omit all cables and shaping, and work to desired length, minus an inch or two for the bottom ribbing. To finish the V-neck, just pick up stitches evenly around and mark the center stitch. Working in the round, on every round, work to 2 stitches before the marked stitch, ssk, knit the center stitch, k2tog, work to the end of the round. Repeat this round until the neckband is the desired depth. Bind off in pattern.

The variation shown was worked in size Large with 9 hanks of Blue Sky Alpacas Melange in the color Salsa. Read about estimating yarn requirements on page 15.

BLITHE TEE

When I was talking to my editor about ideas for customizing, she mentioned upsizing from a little girls' pattern to a woman's. At first I wasn't interested, but then she showed me a picture of a little girl's top that she wanted to make and, after a chuckle, I took on her challenge. The Blithe Tee is the result. The pattern offers both girls' and women's sizes, but more explanation on upsizing is given on page 52.

PATTERN FEATURES
Top-down set-in sleeve construction, provisional cast-on, simple stripe colorwork, picking up and knitting, short-row shaping, ribbing.

SIZES

2 (4, 6, 8, 10) <X-Small (Small, Medium, Large, 1X-Large, 2X-Large, 3X-Large)>

Instructions for girls' sizes are given first; women's sizes are between < >. If only one number is given, it applies to all sizes.

FINISHED MEASUREMENTS

21¾ (24¾, 27¾, 28¼, 30½) <32 (34¼, 36¼, 40¾, 44¼, 48, 52¼)"> chest

YARN

Girls': Reynolds Top Seed Cotton (100% cotton; 105 yards / 50 grams): 2 (3, 3, 4, 4) hanks #4734 Spring Mix (MC); Tahki Stacy Charles Cotton Classic (100% cotton; 108 yards / 50 grams): 1 (2, 2, 2, 2) hanks #3528 Light Bright Yellow (A)

Women's: Stitch Diva Studios Studio Silk (100% silk; 120 yards / 50 grams): 5 (5, 5, 6, 6, 7, 7) hanks Poison Eggplant (MC); 2 (2, 3, 3, 3, 3, 3) hanks Black (A)

NEEDLES

One 24" (60 cm) long or longer circular (circ) needle size US 5 (3.75 mm)

One or two 24" (60 cm) long or longer circular needles or one set of five double-pointed needles sizes US 5 (3.75 mm) and US 4 (3.5 mm), for Sleeves

Change needle size if necessary to obtain correct gauge.

NOTIONS

Crochet hook size US G/6 (4 mm) (optional); waste yarn; removable marker; stitch markers in 3 colors

GAUGE

22 sts and 28 rows = 4" (10 cm) in Stockinette stitch (St st), using larger needle

STITCH PATTERNS

Stripe Pattern

Working in St st (beginning with a knit row if working back and forth), work *4 rows/rnds in MC, then 2 rows/rnds in A; repeat from * for Stripe Pattern. *Note: Carry color not in use along outside edge when working back and forth, and along back of work when working in the rnd. To hide color changes when working in the rnd, work the first rnd in the new color, then slip the first st of the next rnd purlwise, and knit the remaining sts. If working in MC, knit all sts on the next 2 rnds.*

3x1 Rib

(multiple of 4 sts; 1-rnd repeat)
All Rnds: *K3, p1; repeat from * to end.

BACK

Note: After the initial Provisional CO, use Backward Loop CO for any other COs in this pattern (see Special Techniques, page 152).

Using larger circ needle, waste yarn, and Provisional CO, CO 44 (50, 54, 64, 72) <80 (86, 88, 92, 98, 102, 106)> sts. (WS) Change to A; purl 1 row. Change to MC and Stripe Pattern; work even until piece measures 3 (3½, 4, 4½, 4¾) <6 (6¼, 6¾, 6¼, 7, 7¼, 7¼)>" from the beginning, ending with a WS row. Make note of last pattern row worked.

Shape Armhole (RS): Increase 1 st each side this row, then every other row 1 (1, 1, 2, 1) <1 (1, 1, 1, 1, 2, 2)> time(s), as follows: K1, m1, work to last st, m1, k1—48 (54, 58, 70, 76) <84 (90, 92, 96, 102, 108, 112)> sts. Work even for 1 row.

Next Row (RS): CO 2 (3, 2, 2, 2) <2 (2, 4, 4, 2, 3, 4)> sts at beginning of next 2 rows, 4 (4, 3, 2, 2) <0 (0, 0, 4, 3, 4, 6)> sts at beginning of next 2 rows, then 0 (0, 4, 0, 0) <0 (0, 0, 0, 5, 5, 6)> sts at beginning of next 2 rows—60 (68, 76, 78, 84) <88 (94, 100, 112, 122, 132, 144)> sts. Transfer sts to waste yarn for Body. Break yarn.

FRONT

With WS facing, carefully unravel Provisional CO and place sts on larger circ needle. Join A, p12 (14, 16, 18, 20) < 24 (26, 28, 28, 30, 32, 32) >, join a second ball of A, BO center 20 (22, 22, 28, 32) <32 (34, 32, 36, 38, 38, 42)> sts for Back neck, purl to end. Place removable marker for top of shoulder. *Note: If you prefer, you may work each side of the Front separately before joining at the center Front.* (RS) Working BOTH SIDES AT SAME TIME, using separate balls of yarn, change to MC and Stripe Pattern; work even until piece measures 1 (1½, 1½, 2, 2) <3 (3, 3½, 3½, 4, 4, 4)>" from top of shoulder, ending with a WS row.

Shape Neck (RS): Increase 1 st each neck edge this row, then every other row 4 <5 (6, 5, 7, 7, 7, 7)> times, as follows: On right Front, work to last st, m1, k1; on left Front, k1, m1, work to end—17 (19, 21, 23, 25) <30 (33, 34, 36, 38, 40, 40)> sts. Work even for 1 row.

Next Row (RS): Work across right Front, CO 10 (12, 12, 18, 22) <20 (20, 20, 20, 22, 22, 26)> sts for center neck, work across left Front to end, cutting second ball of yarn—44 (50, 54, 64, 72) <80 (86, 88, 92, 98,102, 106)> sts for Front. Work even until piece measures same as for Back from top of shoulder to beginning of armhole shaping, ending with the same row of Stripe Pattern as for Back. Shape armholes as for Back—60 (68, 76, 78, 84) <88 (94, 100, 112, 122, 132, 144)> sts.

BODY

Join Back and Front (RS): Work across Front sts, pm, work across Back sts from waste yarn—120 (136, 152, 156, 168) <176 (188, 200, 224, 244, 264, 288)> sts. Join for working in the rnd; pm for beginning of rnd.

Sizes – (–, –, 8, 10) <–> Only:

Continuing in St st (knit every rnd) and Stripe Pattern, work even for 6 rnds.

Shape Hips: Increase 4 sts this rnd, then every – (–, –, 10, 12) rnds 5 times, as follows: [K1, m1, work to 1 st before marker, m1, k1, sm] twice— – (–, –, 180, 192) sts.

All Sizes:

Next Rnd: Continuing in St st (knit every rnd) and Stripe Pattern, work even until piece measures 7¼ (7¼, 8, 9½, 10¾) < 12¼ (12¼, 12¾, 12½, 11½, 10½, 10½) >" from underarm, ending with second rnd in A. Change to MC; knit 1 rnd.

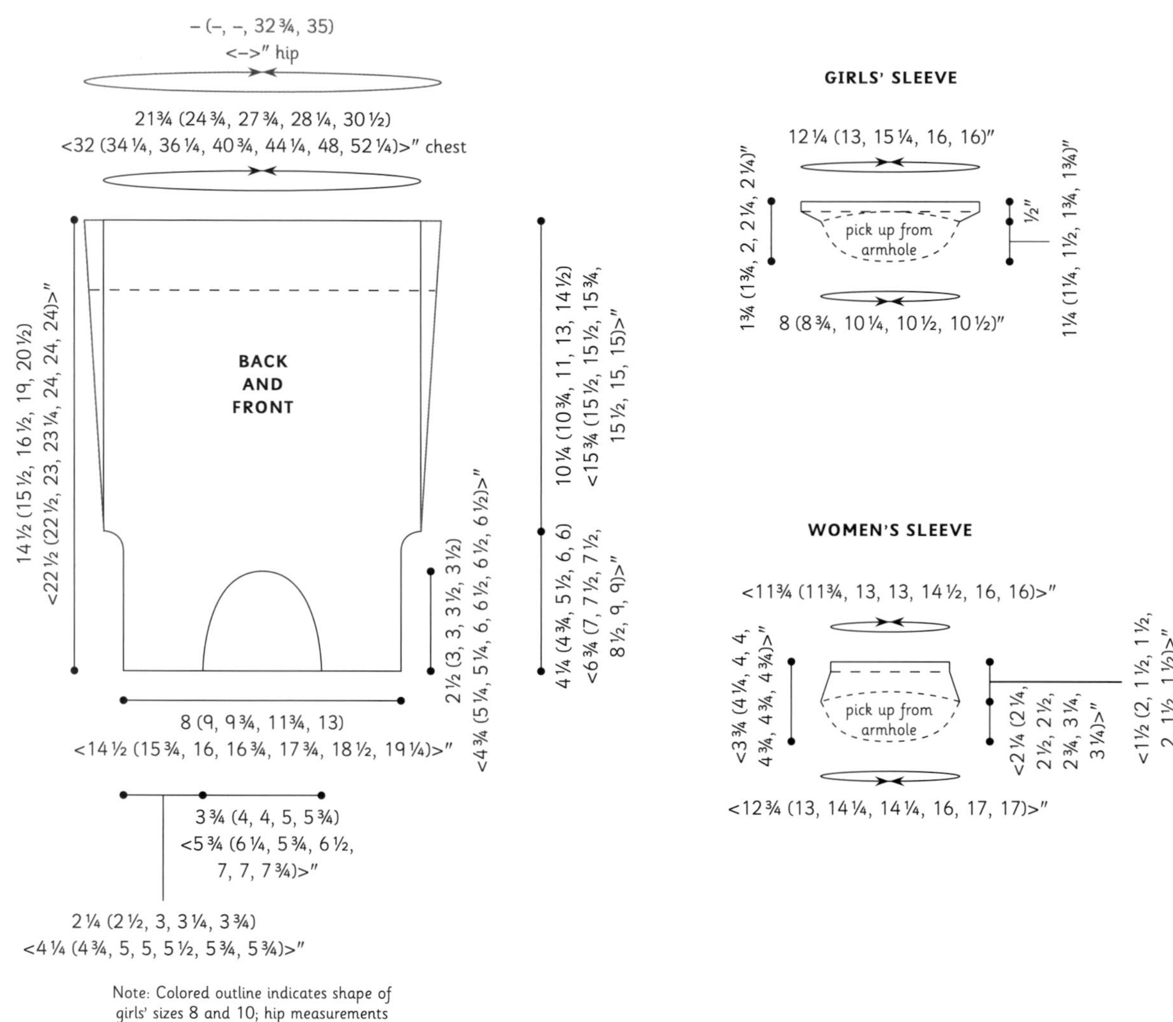

Eyelet Rnd: *K2tog, yo; repeat from * to end. Knit 1 rnd. Change to A and St st; knit 2 rnds. Change to Stripe Pattern; work even until piece measures 9¾ (10¼, 10½, 12½, 14) <15¼ (15, 15, 15¼, 15, 14½, 14½)>" from underarm, ending with second rnd in A. Change to MC and 3x1 Rib; work even for 4 rnds. BO all sts loosely in pattern.

SLEEVES

Note: Use your preferred method of working in the rnd when working the Sleeves (see page 23). You will be using 3 different color markers: 1 color for beginning of rnd, 2 of color A to mark end of cap shaping, and 2 of color B to mark center of cap shaping.

With RS facing, beginning at bottom center of underarm, pick up and knit 44 (48, 56, 58, 58) <70 (72, 78, 78, 88, 94, 94)> sts, as follows: 8 (9, 10, 8, 8) <9 (9, 9, 9, 11, 11, 11)> sts, pm color A, 7 (7, 9, 11, 11) <15 (15, 17, 17, 19, 21, 21)> sts, pm color B, 14 (16, 18, 20, 20) <22 (24, 26, 26, 28, 30, 30)> sts, pm color B, 7 (7, 9, 11, 11) <15 (15, 17, 17, 19, 21, 21)> sts, pm color A, 8 (9, 10, 8, 8) <9 (9, 9, 9, 11, 11, 11)> sts. *Note: Be sure to pick up the same number of sts between bottom center of armhole and top of shoulder on both sides of the armhole. Color B markers should be equidistant from top of shoulder. If you would prefer not to place markers while you pick up sts, you may first pick up the total number of sts required, join for working in the rnd, then knit 1 rnd, placing the markers according to the numbers given in the pick-up instructions.*

Shape Cap

Note: Cap will be shaped using Short Rows (see Special Techniques, page 156). Hide wraps as you come to them.

Row 1 (RS): Working back and forth, begin St st. Work to second color B marker, sm, wrp-t.

Row 2: Repeat Row 1.

Row 3: Work to wrapped st of row before last row worked, work wrapped st, work 1 st, wrp-t.

Repeat Row 3 until you have reached the color A markers on each side of Sleeve, ending with a WS row.

Next Rnd (RS): Change to working in the rnd, hiding remaining wrap as you come to it, and removing all markers; pm for beginning of rnd.

Sizes 2 (4, 6, 8, 10) Only:

Next Rnd: *K1, k1-f/b; repeat from * to last 4 (0, 0, 2, 2) sts, [k1-f/b] 4 (0, 0, 2, 2) times—68 (72, 84, 88, 88) sts. Change to A and 3x1 Rib; work even for 3 rnds. BO all sts loosely in pattern.

Shape Sleeve

Sizes X-Small (Small, Medium, Large, 1X-Large, 2X-Large, 3X-Large) Only:

Next Rnd: Decrease 2 sts this rnd, then every other rnd 2 (3, 2, 2, 3, 2, 2) times, as follows: K1, k2tog, knit to last 3 sts, ssk, k1—64 (64, 72, 72, 80, 88, 88) sts remain. Change to smaller needles, A, and 3x1 Rib; work even for 4 rnds. BO all sts loosely in pattern.

FINISHING

Plain Neckband (shown on Girls' Version): With RS facing, using larger dpns and A, and beginning at center Back, pick up and knit approximately 2 sts for every 3 rows, and 1 st in every CO st around neck opening. Join for working in the rnd; pm for beginning of rnd. Knit 1 rnd. BO all sts loosely purlwise. Using crochet hook and A, work single crochet into each knit st (optional). Fasten off.

Ribbed Neckband (shown on Women's Version): With RS facing, using smaller dpns and A, and beginning at center Back, pick up and knit approximately 2 sts for every 3 rows, and 1 st in every CO st around neck opening, making sure to end with a multiple of 4 sts. Join for working in the rnd; pm for beginning of rnd. Begin 3x1 Rib; work even for 4 rnds. BO all sts loosely in pattern.

Twisted Cord Tie: Cut 2 strands of MC 6 times hip measurement. Holding 2 strands together, fold strands in half and secure one end to a stationary object. Twist from other end until it begins to buckle. Fold twisted length in half and, holding ends together, allow to twist up on itself. Tie cut end in an overhand knot to secure. Detach from stationary object and tie overhand knot to secure.

Thread Twisted Cord Tie through eyelets (see photo on page 81).

Block as desired.

MAKE IT YOUR OWN

Since this pattern is so basic, you can lower or raise the neckline by knitting fewer or more rows before shaping it, or change the sleeves completely. For a top that looks more traditional, add waist shaping or omit the eyelets and shorten the length slightly.

CHAPTER 4

Tailored Raglans: Customizing for a Perfect Fit

Although raglans are simple and straight-forward to knit, they can be a little tricky to customize if you need extra room in the chest or less width in the sleeves, which is why some people wind up with ill-fitting raglans (and why raglans have a bad reputation in some circles.) But this doesn't have to be the case. In this chapter, I provide guidelines for tweaking raglans for a perfect fit. To build your customizing skills, start with a basic pattern, like Poolside on page 95 or the Zuma Tunic on page 103.

CUSTOMIZING A RAGLAN SWEATER

Almost all top-down sweater constructions are pretty easy to customize because there are no real "rules" for increasing and decreasing while working the upper body (i.e., if you decide to omit or add shaping at any given point, the shaping lines along the armholes or neckline won't be affected). The top-down raglan, however, is another story. With its telltale diagonal lines that run between the upper neck to the underarm, it is one of the most popular top-down sweater styles, though it is probably one of the toughest constructions to customize for fit. And because it's tricky to customize, the top-down raglan seems to get a bum rap. I hope to defuse this bad reputation by showing you some customizing tips that will help you create a raglan fitted to your body.

So What Makes a Top-Down Raglan So Hard to Customize?

When you knit or design a raglan, you are basically making a rectangle of fabric with four diagonal lines that flow from the tops of the shoulders to the underarms, with a neck opening in its center (see illustration below). In order to create these diagonal lines, a typical raglan pattern will tell you to increase the stitches on the body and sleeves at the exact same rate—every right-side row at eight key spots, on either side of each of the four markers. The rate of increasing is the same on the two front/sleeves and back/sleeves—so the proportional width at any point between the neck and the underarms remains the same.

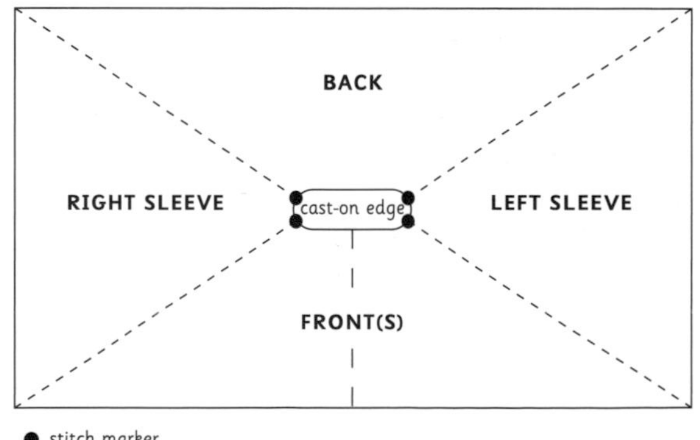

This can create fit problems because A) since our bodies are unique, not everyone can wear a perfect rectangle over their shoulders and have it fit like a dream, and B) when you follow these increases blindly until the chest circumference is achieved, you may find that certain parts of the sweater end up being too large, while other parts end up being too small, depending on your particular body type. For example, if you have a large bust and small upper arms, in order for you to obtain a circumference that is guaranteed to fit around your chest, you may end up with sleeves that are too large for you. And, since you are adding the same number of stitches at each designated point at regular intervals, it will take you more intervals to get to your desired circumference, meaning you may also end up with an armhole that is way too deep for you.

Although there are some pretty distinct rules for creating standard raglan seams, it is possible to alter the pattern for a nicer fitting result. The first step is to take a look at the pattern's schematic and compare it to your desired chest circumference and underarm depth. Also take note of the circumference of the upper sleeve—not all schematics will show you this, so if yours doesn't, look through the pattern and make note of the number of sleeve stitches you will have on the needles once all the stitches are increased, including any extra stitches that are added for the underarm/body, then divide this number by the stitch gauge to find out the sleeve circumference. If all three points work for you—the chest circumference, the sleeve depth and sleeve circumference—it's your lucky day! Work the pattern as written. Chances are, however, you'll need to make some adjustments. Be aware that when you make these simple adjustments, stitch counts will differ from those in the pattern. But never fear! If you require certain multiples of stitches to accommodate a stitch pattern, keep track of your personal stitch counts and anticipate required multiples so you can make some hidden increases or decreases before you get there. Meanwhile, here are some tips for customizing the fit of that simple-but-oh-so-problematic raglan:

Sleeve Too Roomy?

If the pattern, as written, will produce sleeves that are too large, use these methods to give them a closer fit:

✦ Cast on fewer sleeve stitches at the beginning than the pattern suggests.

✦ Work increases for raglan shaping as directed to a couple of inches before the increases are complete. Then, work increases for the sleeves on every fourth row or round instead of every other row or round, while continuing to increase as instructed for the front and back. Which means, on a top-down raglan pullover, on the rows where you don't work sleeve increases, you will increase 1 stitch on the front, slip your marker, and knit across all sleeve stitches without increasing, then, slip your marker, increase the first back stitch, and then at the other end, increase another back stitch, slip the marker, and then work across the sleeve with no increases, and continue on.

✦ Once you have completed the body and are ready to work the sleeves, pick up and knit fewer stitches than are called for in the underarm section.

Chest Too Small?

With raglans, each section—front, back and sleeves—typically grows at the same rate. So, if you create a sleeve that fits you perfectly, but the chest will then be too small, you might be tempted to continue increasing until the chest fits. If you do this, you might find that not only will the sleeves be too large, but the armhole depth will be too long as well. One way to deal with this effectively is to simply work double increases in the front and back sections. Just work the pattern as instructed to a few inches above the end of the armhole. Then, instead of working an increase as written in the front and back sections, work two increases. For example, the pattern may state the following: "K1, m1 [sleeve increase], work to 1 st before marker, m1 [sleeve increase], k1, sm, k1, m1 [back increase], work to one st before second marker, m1 [back increase], k1, sm, k1, m1 [sleeve increase], work to 1 st before third marker, m1 [sleeve increase], k1, sm, k1, m1 [front increase], work to 1 st before end of rnd, m1, k1." Instead, work increases like this: "K1, m1 [sleeve increase], work to 1 st before marker, m1 [sleeve increase], k1, sm, [k1, m1] twice [back increases], work to 2 sts before second marker, [m1, k1] twice [back increases], sm, k1, m1 [sleeve increase], work to 1 st before third marker, m1 [sleeve increase], k1, sm, [k1, m1] twice [front increases], work to last 2 sts, [m1, k1] twice [front increases]". *Note: In this instance you will have added 4 extra stitches to each front and back instead of 2. You can work double increases for a couple of inches before the end of the armhole without it being too noticeable.*

Chest Too Roomy?

If the pattern, as written, will produce a chest that is too large, give this a whirl:

Work the pattern as written, but stop increasing for front and back on every other row a few inches before reaching the desired length of the yoke section. Instead, work front and back increases on every fourth row until the sleeve increases are complete (see first section for details).

Armhole Too Deep?

Another problem with raglans is that when the row gauge is more than one or two rows larger than the stitch gauge, the length of the garment grows at a greater rate than the width. This sometimes leaves the knitter with horrifyingly deep armholes. Making an adjustment to fix too-deep armholes is easy. First, make sure that your row gauge matches the one in the pattern, then check the schematic for your size. If the armhole is deeper than you like, but the rest of the final stitch counts will work for you, you can follow the pattern to a few inches shorter than where you want your armhole to land. Then, work double increases into each of the sections until you have reached the required number of stitches. An alternative would be to work some increases on every round rather than every other round so that by the time you have the required number of stitches, you will have worked fewer rounds and have a shorter armhole.

SIZES

XX-Small (X-Small, Small, Medium, Large, 1X-Large, 2X-Large, 3X-Large)

FINISHED CIRCUMFERENCE

31¼ (33, 35¾, 39¼, 41, 43¾, 47¼, 51¾)"

YARN

Berroco Ultra Alpaca (50% super fine alpaca / 50% Peruvian wool; 215 yards / 100 grams): 7 (7, 7, 8, 8, 9, 9, 10) hanks #6284 Plum Mix (MC); 1 hank each #6268 Candied Yam Mix (A) and #6274 Winter Squash (B)

NEEDLES

One 32" (80 cm) long or longer circular (circ) needle size US 8 (5 mm)

One or two 24" (60 cm) long or longer circular needles or one set of five double-pointed needles (dpn) size US 8 (5 mm), as preferred, for Sleeves

One 32" (80 cm) long or longer circular needle size US 7 (4.5 mm)

One 32" (80 cm) long or longer circular needle size US 6 (4 mm)

Change needle size if necessary to obtain correct gauge.

NOTIONS

Crochet hook size US 7 (4.5 mm); stitch markers; waste yarn; seven ⅝–1" buttons (optional; instructions for crocheted buttons included); one size 10 black sew-on snap; tapestry needle

GAUGE

18 sts and 22 rows = 4" (10 cm) in Stockinette stitch (St st), using larger needle

GARLAND

This saucy sweater-coat is the perfect solution for those in-between days when a heavy coat is too much and a regular cardigan isn't enough. Knit from the top down with raglan shaping and lots of color, this coat has a versatile collar that can be worn snapped closed for a fashion forward look, or unsnapped for a more casual look. The crocheted buttons are a lot of fun, but if that look isn't for you, substitute with snaps or opt for a self-tie belt.

PATTERN FEATURES

Top-down raglan construction, picking up and knitting, simple color changes, ribbing.

STITCH PATTERNS

1x1 Rib

(odd number of sts; 2-row repeat)
Row 1 (RS): K1, *p1, k1; repeat from * to end.
Row 2: P1, *k1, p1; repeat from * to end.
Repeat Rows 1 and 2 for 1x1 Rib.

2x2 Rib

(multiple of 4 sts + 2; 2-row repeat)
Row 1 (WS): P2, *k2, p2; repeat from * to end.
Row 2: K2, *p2, k2; repeat from * to end.
Repeat Rows 1 and 2 for 2x2 Rib.

YOKE

Using largest 32"-long circ needle and MC, CO 1 st for Left Front, pm, 6 (6, 8, 6, 6, 8, 8, 8) sts for Left Sleeve, pm, 26 (26, 28, 30, 30, 32, 34, 38) sts for Back, pm, 6 (6, 8, 6, 6, 8, 8, 8) sts for Right Sleeve, pm, and 1 st for Right Front—40 (40, 46, 44, 44, 50, 52, 56) sts. Begin St st, beginning with a purl row; work even for 1 row.

Shape Yoke and Front Neck

Increase Row 1 (RS): K1-f/b, sm, [k1-f/b, knit to 1 st before marker, k1-f/b, sm] 3 times, k1-f/b—48 (48, 54, 52, 52, 58, 60, 64) sts. Work even for 1 row.

Increase Row 2 (RS): [K1-f/b] twice, sm, [k1-f/b, knit to 1 st before marker, k1-f/b, sm] 3 times, [k1-f/b] twice—58 (58, 64, 62, 62, 68, 70, 74) sts. Work even for 1 row.

Increase Row 3 (RS): Increase 10 sts this row, then every other row 9 (9, 10, 11, 13, 12, 13, 15) times, as follows: sm: [K1-f/b, knit to 1 st before marker, k1-f/b, sm] 4 times, k1-f/b, knit to last st, k1-f/b—158 (158, 174, 182, 202, 198, 210, 234) sts. Work even for 1 row.

SHAPE YOKE

Increase Row 4 (RS): Increase 8 sts this row, then every other row 7 (8, 8, 8, 6, 9, 8, 8) times, as follows: [Knit to 1 st before marker, k1-f/b, sm, k1-f/b] 4 times, knit to end—222 (230, 246, 254, 258, 278, 282, 306) sts. Work even for 1 row.

BODY

Next Row (RS): Knit across 32 (33, 35, 37, 39, 40, 41, 45) sts of Left Front, transfer next 46 (48, 52, 52, 52, 58, 58, 62) sts to waste yarn for Left Sleeve, removing markers, CO 2 (4, 6, 10, 12, 14, 20, 22) sts for underarm, knit across 66 (68, 72, 76, 76, 82, 84, 92) sts of Back, transfer next 46 (48, 52, 52, 52, 58, 58, 62) to waste yarn for Right Sleeve, removing markers, CO 2 (4, 6, 10, 12, 14, 20, 22) sts for underarm, knit across 32 (33, 35, 37, 39, 40, 41, 45) sts of Right Front—134 (142, 154, 170, 178, 190, 206, 226) sts. Working back and forth, work even until piece measures 6 (6¼, 5¾, 6, 6½, 6¼, 6¾, 6)" from underarm, ending with a WS row, and decreasing 1 st on last row—133 (141, 153, 169, 177, 189, 205, 225) sts remain.

Next Row (RS): Change to size US 7 32"-long circ needle and 1x1 Rib; work even for 6", ending with a WS row. Change to largest 32"-long needle and St st; work even until piece measures 21½ (22¼, 21¾, 21½, 21½, 21¾, 21¾, 21)" from underarm, increasing 1 st on first row and ending with a WS row —134 (142, 154, 170, 178, 190, 206, 226) sts. Purl 1 row (turning row). Change to smallest 32"-long circ needle; work in St st for 6 rows. BO all sts loosely purlwise.

SLEEVES

Note: Use your preferred method of working in the rnd for the Sleeves (see page 23).

Transfer Sleeve sts from waste yarn to largest needle(s). With RS facing, join MC at underarm; begin St st, work to end, pick up and knit 1 (2, 3, 5, 6, 7, 10, 11) st(s) from st(s) CO for underarm, pm for beginning of rnd, pick up and knit 1 (2, 3, 5, 6, 7, 10, 11) st(s) from st(s) CO for underarm—48 (52, 58, 62, 64, 72, 78, 84) sts. Knit 5 rnds.

Shape Sleeve: Decrease 2 sts this rnd, every 7 (6, 5, 5, 4, 4, 3, 3) rnds 7 (7, 4, 3, 12, 3, 14, 12) times, then every 0 (5, 4, 4, 3, 3, 2, 2) rnds 0 (2, 8, 10, 2, 14, 6, 9) times, as follows: K1, k2tog, knit to last 3 sts, ssk, k1—32 (32, 32, 34, 34, 36, 36, 40) sts. Work even until piece measures 12 (12½, 12½, 13, 13, 13, 13, 13)" from underarm, or to 6" from desired length. Change to size US 7 needle(s) and 1x1 Rib; work even for 6". BO all sts loosely in pattern.

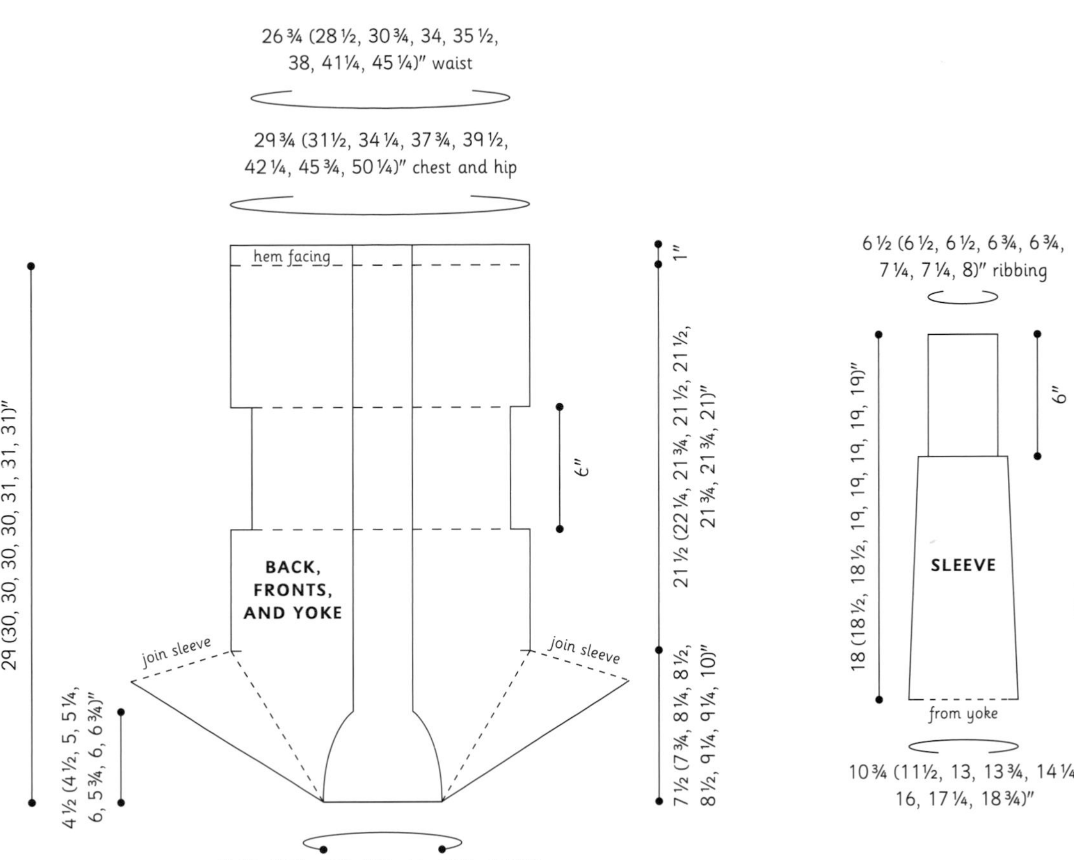

BELT

Using size US 7 needle, CO 15 sts.

Row 1 (RS): Slip 1 purlwise wyif, *p1, k1; repeat from * to end.

Row 2: Slip 1 purlwise wyib, *k1, p1; repeat from * to end.

Repeat Rows 1 and 2 until piece measures 60 (62, 64, 66, 70, 74, 78, 82)" or to desired length from the beginning. BO all sts loosely in pattern.

FINISHING

Fold hem to WS at turning row and sew to WS, being careful not to let sts show on RS.

Button Band: With RS facing, using size US 7 needle and MC, beginning at base of Left Front neck shaping, pick up and knit an odd number of sts along Left Front edge. Begin 1x1 Rib, beginning with Row 2; work even for 1½", ending with a WS row. BO all sts loosely knitwise.

Buttonhole Band: Place markers for buttons on Right Front, the first 1½" from the base of neck shaping, the last 3" from the bottom edge, and the remaining 5 evenly spaced between. Work as for Button Band until Band measures ½", ending with a WS row. Buttonhole Row (RS): Work to first buttonhole marker, *BO 2 sts, work to next marker; repeat from * to last marker, BO 2 sts, work to end. Work even until Band measures 1½", ending with a WS row, CO 2 sts over BO sts on first row using Backward Loop CO (see Special Techniques, page 152). BO all sts loosely knitwise. Sew buttons opposite buttonholes.

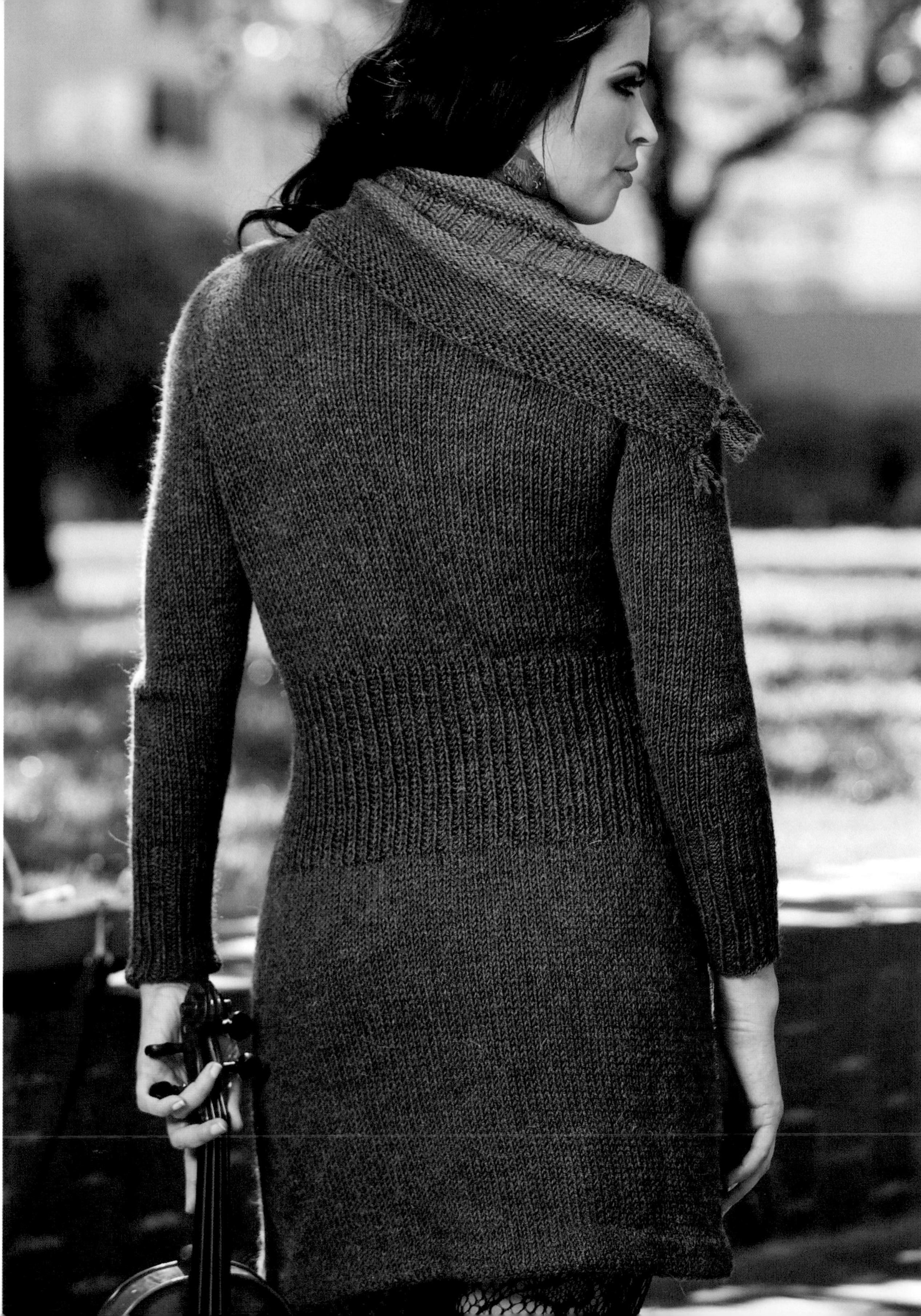

Collar: With RS *facing*, using largest circ needle and MC, beginning at BO edge of Buttonhole Band and ending at raglan "seam" between Left Sleeve and Left Front, pick up and knit a multiple of 4 sts + 2. Begin 2x2 Rib; work even for 2", ending with a WS row. Change to A; work even for 1", ending with a WS row. Change to B; work even for 2 rows. Change to MC and Garter st (knit every row); work even for 1½", ending with a WS row. Change to A and St st; work even for 1", ending with a WS row. Change to MC and Garter st; work even for 4 rows. Change to A and 2x2 Rib; work even for 1½", ending with a WS row. Change to B; work even for 2 rows. Change to MC and Garter st; work even for 4 rows. Change to A and St st; work even for 1", ending with a WS row. Change to MC; work even for 1½", ending with a WS row. Change to MC and Garter st; work even for 1", ending with a WS row. BO all sts loosely knitwise.

Collar Fringe: Using 4 strands of MC 4" long for each fringe, beginning just above pick-up row of Collar on Right Front, work fringe in approximately ¾" intervals along side edge of Collar, as follows: Fold strands in half; with WS of piece facing, insert crochet hook just above edge to receive fringe, from back to front; catch the folded strands of yarn with the hook and pull through work to form a loop, insert ends of yarn through loop and pull to tighten.

Sew opposite side edge of Collar along Left Front neck edge, ending at BO edge of Button Band, easing Collar as necessary to fit. Sew one half of snap to WS of Collar, approximately 3½" above pick-up edge, along fringed edge. Sew other half of snap along Left Front neck edge, approximately 1½" below raglan "seam." Adjust placement if desired, so that Collar fits comfortably (see photo).

CROCHET BUTTONS (make 7)

Using MC and crochet hook, make a slipknot, leaving 12" long or longer tail, and place on crochet hook.

Rnd 1: Ch 5, sl st into first st to make loop.

Rnd 2: Ch 1 into first ch st, 2 sc into each st to end, sl st into first ch st to join—10 sts, including first ch st.

Rnd 3: Ch 1, sc into first st, 2 sc into each sc to end, sl st into first ch st—20 sts.

Rnd 4: *[Insert hook into next sc, pull loop up] 4 times (5 loops on hook); yo hook, pull loop through all loops; repeat from * to end. Fasten off and cut yarn, leaving 10" tail. Thread tail through tapestry needle. Stuff tail from slipknot into center of button. Thread tapestry needle through sc rnd (Rnd 2) to close bottom of button. Fasten off, but do not cut tail. Using tail, sew buttons opposite buttonholes.

Block as desired.

MAKE IT YOUR OWN

For a wide collar that lies centered around the shoulders, simply pick up stitches evenly around the neckline and knit as instructed. For a much shorter sporty sweater, bind off all Body stitches after the waist ribbing.

POOLSIDE

Knit a sweater to wear with your bikini? Why not! When my first book, *Custom Knits,* came out, many knitters wondered why so many of the models were wearing sweaters over their bathing suits. Truth be told, even on a warm summer day in California, the air can get chilly when the sun starts to set. So a sweater-bikini combo, in my opinion, is a perfect match. And Poolside is one of those knits that can do double duty as either a cover-up or a springtime pullover.

SIZES

X-Small (Small, Medium, Large, 1X-Large, 2X-Large, 3X-Large)

FINISHED MEASUREMENTS

30 (34, 36, 40, 44, 48, 52)" chest, after blocking

YARN

Knit One Crochet Too 2nd Time Cotton (75% recycled cotton / 25% acrylic; 180 yards / 100 grams): 4 (5, 5, 6, 7, 7, 8) hanks #913 Granite

NEEDLES

One 29" (70 cm) long or longer circular (circ) needle size US 7 (4.5 mm)

One or two 24" (60 cm) long or longer circular needles or one set of five double-pointed needles (dpn) size US 7 (4.5 mm), as preferred, for Sleeves

Change needle size if necessary to obtain correct gauge.

NOTIONS

Stitch markers; waste yarn

GAUGE

16 sts and 24 rows = 4" (10 cm) in Stockinette stitch (St st), after blocking

YOKE

Using 29"-long or longer circ needle, CO 2 sts for left Front, pm, 2 sts for Left Sleeve, pm, 18 (20, 20, 24, 26, 30, 34) for Back, 2 sts for Right Sleeve, pm, 2 sts for right Front—26 (28, 28, 32, 34, 38, 42) sts. Begin Andalusian Stitch (worked flat); work even for 1 row.

Note: Raglan and Neck Shaping are worked at the same time; please read entire section through before beginning. Neck shaping will not be completed until Sleeves are divided and Fronts and Back are joined for Body.

Shape Raglan (RS): Continuing in Andalusian Stitch, and working increased sts in pattern as they become available, increase 8 sts this row, then every other row 17 (19, 21, 23, 25, 28, 29) times, as follows: [Work to 1 st before marker, m1, k1, sm, m1] 4 times, work to end. AT THE SAME TIME, beginning on fourth RS row, shape neck as follows:

PATTERN FEATURES

Top-down raglan construction, incorporating simple stitch pattern into increases, picking up and knitting, ribbing.

STITCH PATTERNS

Andalusian Stitch (worked flat)

(even number of sts; 4-row repeat)
Row 1 (WS): Purl.
Row 2: Knit.
Row 3: *K1, p1; repeat from * to end.
Row 4: Purl.
Repeat Rows 1–4 for Andalusian Stitch (worked flat).

Andalusian Stitch (worked in the rnd)

(even number of sts; 4-rnd repeat)
Rnds 1 and 2: Knit.
Rnd 3: *P1, k1; repeat from * to end.
Rnd 4: Knit.
Repeat Rnds 1–4 for Andalusian Stitch (worked in the rnd).

Shape Neck (RS): Continuing raglan shaping as established, increase 1 st at beginning and end of this row, then every 7 (7, 7, 6, 6, 5, 4) rows 6 (7, 7, 9, 10, 12, 14) times, working increases as k1-f/b on RS rows and p1-f/b on WS rows. When raglan shaping is complete [38 (42, 46, 50, 54, 60, 62) sts each Sleeve; 54 (60, 64, 72, 78, 88, 94) sts for Back], work Body as follows:

BODY

Divide Sleeves and Join Back and Fronts (RS): Continuing st pattern and neck shaping as established, work to first marker, remove marker, transfer next 38 (42, 46, 50, 54, 60, 62) sts to waste yarn for Left Sleeve, remove marker, CO 3 (4, 4, 4, 5, 4, 5) sts for underarm, pm for side, CO 3 (4, 4, 4, 5, 4, 5) sts for underarm, work to next marker, remove marker, transfer next 38 (42, 46, 50, 54, 60, 62) sts to waste yarn for Right Sleeve, remove marker, CO 3 (4, 4, 4, 5, 4, 5) sts for underarm, pm for side, CO 3 (4, 4, 4, 5, 4, 5) sts for underarm, work to end. Do not join. Working back and forth, work even until neck shaping is complete, ending with a WS row. Break yarn.

Join Fronts (RS): With RS facing, transfer 30 (34, 36, 40, 44, 48, 52) left Front sts to left-hand end of needle, removing marker, so that sts are now in the following order, with RS facing: Back, right Front, left Front. Rejoin yarn to Back sts. Work across Back, right Front, then left Front sts—120 (136, 144, 160, 176, 192, 208) sts. Join for working in the rnd; pm for beginning of rnd. Change to Andalusian Stitch (worked in the rnd), beginning with rnd after last row of Andalusian Stitch (worked flat). Work even until piece measures 6 ¼ (6 ¼, 6, 5 ¾, 5 ¾, 5, 4 ¾)" from underarm, ending with Rnd 1 or 3 of pattern.

Shape Waist: Decrease 4 sts this rnd, then every 6 rnds twice, as follows: [K1, k2tog, sm, work to 3 sts before marker, ssk, k1] twice—108 (124, 132, 148, 164, 180, 196) sts remain. Work even for 5 rnds.

Shape Hip: Increase 4 sts this rnd, then every 6 rnds twice, as follows: [K1, m1, work to 1 st before marker, m1, k1, sm] twice—120 (136, 144, 160, 176, 192, 208) sts. Work even until piece measures 15 ¾ (16 ¼, 15 ½, 15 ¼, 15 ¼, 14 ¼, 13 ¾)" from underarm.

Shape Slit (RS): K4, work in Andalusian Stitch (worked flat) to 4 sts before next marker, beginning with row following last rnd of Andalusian Stitch (worked in the rnd), k4, turn; place remaining 60 (68, 72, 80, 88, 96, 104) sts on waste yarn for Front. Working back and forth on Back sts only, and working first and last 4 sts of every row in Garter st (knit every row) and center sts in pattern as established, work even until slit measures approximately 4", ending with Row 3 of pattern.

Next Row (RS): K4, knit the knit sts and purl the purl sts to the last 4 sts, k4. Work even for 1", working first and last 4 sts in Garter st, and center sts in 1x1 Rib as established. BO all sts in pattern. With RS facing, rejoin yarn to Front sts and work as for Back slit.

SLEEVES

Note: Use your preferred method of working in the rnd when working the Sleeves (see page 23).

Transfer Sleeve sts from waste yarn to needle(s). With RS facing, beginning at center of underarm, pick up and knit 3 (4, 4, 4, 5, 4, 5) sts from CO sts for underarm, work in pattern to end, pick up and knit 3 (4, 4, 4, 5, 4, 5) sts from CO sts for underarm—44 (50, 54, 58, 64, 68, 72) sts. Join for working in the rnd; pm for beginning of rnd. Work even for 5 rnds.

Shape Sleeve: Decrease 2 sts this rnd, then every 10 (9, 9, 9, 9, 9, 7) rnds 4 (5, 5, 5, 5, 5, 6) times, as follows: K1, k2tog, work to last 3 sts, ssk, k1—34 (38, 42, 46, 52, 56, 58) sts remain. Work even until piece measures 16 (16, 16, 16, 16 ½, 16 ½, 16 ½)" from pick-up rnd.

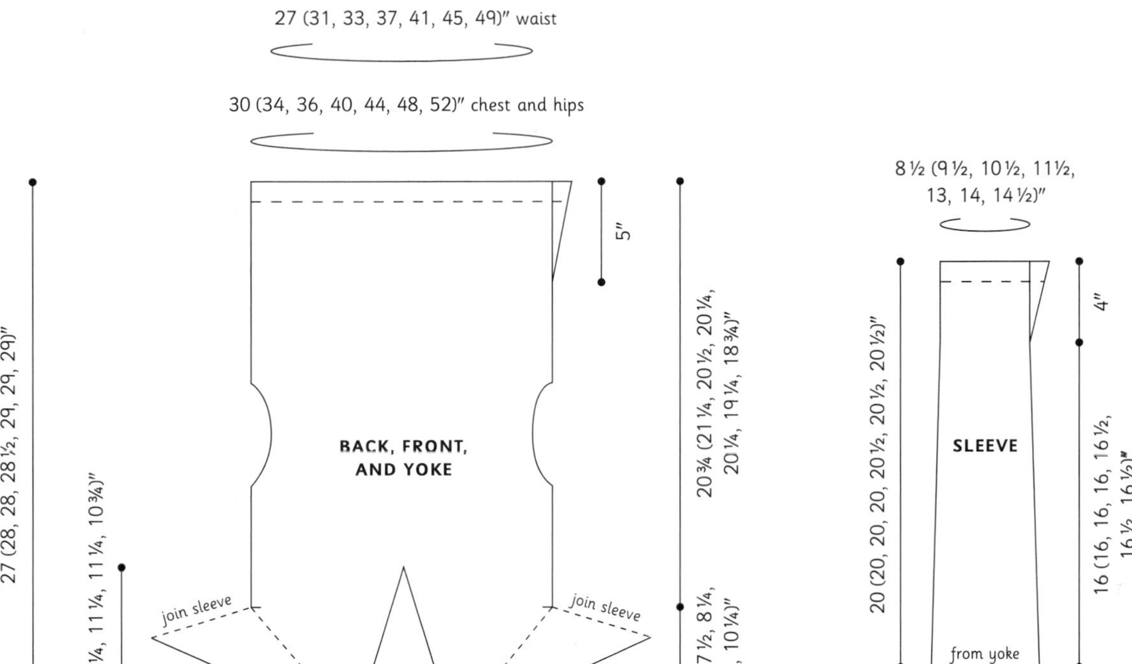

Shape Slit (RS): K4, work in Andalusian Stitch (worked flat) to last 4 sts, beginning with row following last rnd of Andalusian Stitch (worked in the rnd), k4. Working back and forth, and working first and last 4 sts of every row in Garter st and center sts in pattern as established, work even for approximately 3", ending with Row 3 of pattern.

Next Row (RS): K4, knit the knit sts and purl the purl sts to the last 4 sts, k4. Work even for 1", working first and last 4 sts in Garter st, and center sts in 1x1 Rib as established. BO all sts in pattern.

FINISHING

Neckband: With RS facing, using shorter circ needle, beginning at center back Neck, pick up and knit sts around neck opening. Knit 1 rnd. BO all sts loosely knitwise.

Block as desired.

MAKE IT YOUR OWN

If the neckline shown here is a bit too low, you can raise it by increasing the Front Neck stitches at a faster rate. Have fun with the sleeve length by changing it to three-quarter, elbow, short, or capped.

SIZES

X-Small (Small, Medium, Large, 1X-Large, 2X-Large, 3X-Large)

FINISHED MEASUREMENTS

32 (34¼, 36¼, 40, 42¼, 48, 50½)" chest

YARN

Sirdar Snuggly Baby Bamboo (80% bamboo / 20% wool; 105 yards / 50 grams): 6 (7, 7, 8, 8, 9, 9) #152 Honeybun

NEEDLES

One 29" (70 cm) long or longer circular (circ) needle size US 6 (4 mm)

One 29" (70 cm) long or longer circular needle size US 3 (3.25 mm)

One 24" (60 cm) long or longer circular needle size US 3 (3.25 mm), for neckband

One or two 24" (60 cm) long or longer circular needles or one set of five double-pointed needles (dpn) size US 6 (4 mm), as preferred, for Sleeves

One or two 24" (60 cm) long or longer circular needles or one set of five double-pointed needles (dpn) size US 3 (3.25 mm), as preferred, for Sleeves

Change needle size if necessary to obtain correct gauge.

NOTIONS

Removable markers; waste yarn

GAUGE

22 sts and 28 rows = 4" (10 cm) in Stockinette stitch (St st), using larger needles

ZIGZAG PULLOVER

Worked from the top down, this square neckline blouson pullover is quick and simple. I have to admit, I normally add waist shaping when I knit a sweater—especially a sexy one like this—but the bamboo fiber in the yarn I used begged for a blousy effect, so I omitted the shaping, which left a bit of pouf just above the ribbing on the sleeves and waistband. If you don't want pouf—and there are days when I don't want any, either—you can add some gentle waist shaping. Just take a look at page 21 for some tips on how to do it.

PATTERN FEATURES

Top-down raglan construction, simple stitch pattern, picking up and knitting, ribbing.

STITCH PATTERNS

Zigzag Lace

(multiple of 8 sts; 14-rnd repeat)

Rnd 1: *K6, k2tog, yo; repeat from * to end.

Rnd 2: *K5, k2tog, yo, k1; repeat from * to end.

Rnd 3: *K4, k2tog, yo, k2; repeat from * to end.

Rnd 4: *K3, k2tog, yo, k3; repeat from * to end.

Rnd 5: *K2, k2tog, yo, k4; repeat from * to end.

Rnd 6: *K1, k2tog, yo, k5; repeat from * to end.

Rnd 7: *K2tog, yo, k6; repeat from * to end.

Rnd 8: *Yo, ssk, k6; repeat from * to end.

Rnd 9: *K1, yo, ssk, k5; repeat from * to end.

Rnd 10: *K2, yo, ssk, k4; repeat from * to end.

Rnd 11: *K3, yo, ssk, k3; repeat from * to end.

Rnd 12: *K4, yo, ssk, k2; repeat from * to end.

Rnd 13: *K5, yo, ssk, k1; repeat from * to end.

Rnd 14: *K6, yo, ssk; repeat from * to end.

Repeat Rnds 1–14 for Zigzag Lace.

1x1 Rib

(multiple of 2 sts; 1-rnd repeat)

All Rnds: *K1, p1; repeat from * to end.

YOKE

Using larger circ needle, CO 2 (2, 2, 2, 4, 6, 6) sts for right Front, pm, 6 (6, 8, 8, 8, 4, 4) sts for Right Sleeve, pm, 26 (32, 32, 36, 38, 42, 44) sts for Back, 6 (6, 8, 8, 8, 4, 4) sts for Left Sleeve, pm, 2 (2, 2, 2, 4, 6, 6) sts for left Front—42 (48, 52, 56, 62, 62, 64) sts. (WS) Begin St st, beginning with a purl row; work even for 1 row.

Shape Yoke (RS): Increase 8 sts this row, then every other row 22 (23, 25, 26, 26, 29, 31) times, as follows: [Knit to 1 st before marker, k1-f/b, sm, k1-f/b] 4 times, knit to end—226 (240, 260, 272, 278, 302, 320) sts.

BODY

Next Row (RS): Knit across 25 (26, 28, 29, 31, 36, 38) sts of left Front, transfer next 52 (54, 60, 62, 62, 64, 68) sts to waste yarn for Left Sleeve, removing markers, CO 5 (6, 7, 10, 9, 12, 13) sts for underarm, pm for side, CO 6 (6, 7, 10, 10, 13, 14) sts for underarm, knit across 72 (80, 84, 90, 92, 102, 108) sts of Back, transfer next 52 (54, 60, 62, 62, 64, 68) sts to waste yarn for Right Sleeve, removing markers, CO 11 (12, 14, 20, 19, 25, 27) sts for underarm, knit across 25 (26, 28, 29, 31, 36, 38) sts of

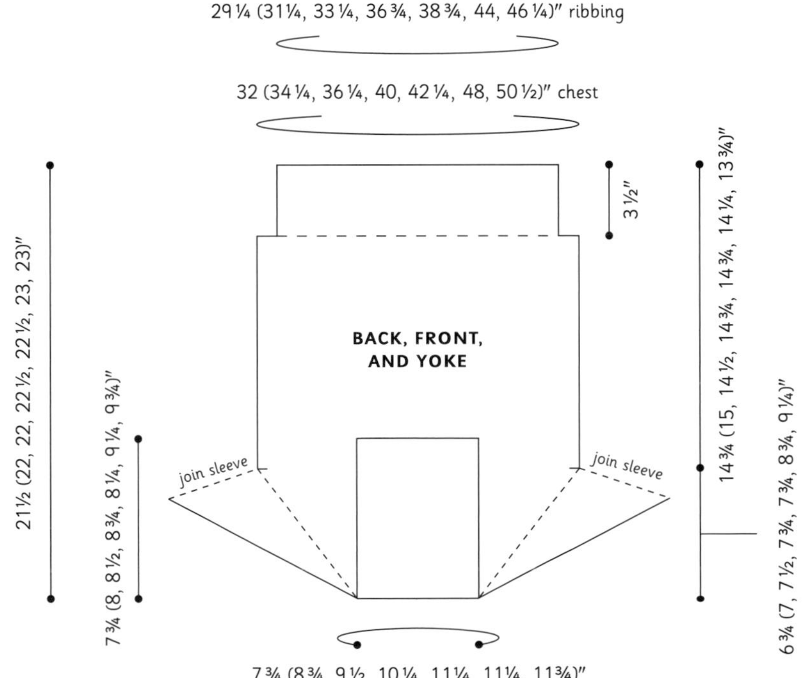

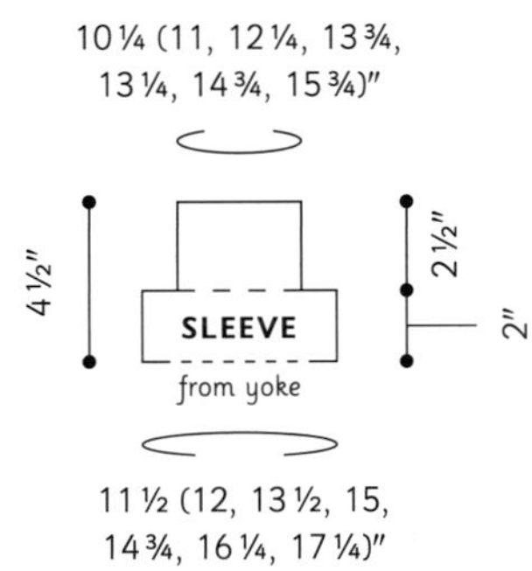

right Front—144 (156, 168, 188, 192, 224, 238) sts. Working back and forth, work even for 7 (7, 7, 7, 3, 3, 3) rows.

Join Fronts (RS): Knit to end, pm, CO 32 (32, 32, 32, 40, 40, 40) sts for center neck, pm, join for working in the rnd, knit across left Front to side marker (now beginning of rnd marker)—176 (188, 200, 220, 232, 264, 278) sts.

Next Rnd: Knit to second marker, work Zigzag Lace to next marker, knit to end. Work even until piece measures 11¼ (11½, 11, 11¼, 11¼, 10¾, 10¼)" from underarm. Change to smaller needles and 1x1 Rib; work even for 3½", removing all markers except beginning of rnd marker on first rnd. BO all sts loosely in pattern.

SLEEVES

Note: Use your preferred method of working in the rnd when working the Sleeves (see page 23).

Transfer Sleeve sts from waste yarn to larger needle(s). With RS facing, join yarn at underarm; begin St st, work to end, pick up and knit 5 (6, 7, 10, 9, 12, 13) sts from sts CO for underarm, pm for beginning of rnd, pick up and knit 6 (6, 7, 10, 10, 13, 14) sts from sts CO for underarm—63 (66, 74, 82, 81, 89, 95) sts. Join for working in the rnd; work even for 14 rnds, decrease 1 (0, 0, 0, 1, 1, 1) st(s) on last rnd—62 (66, 74, 82, 80, 88, 94) sts remain. Change to smaller needles and 1x1 Rib; work even for 2½". BO all sts loosely in pattern.

FINISHING

Neckband: Using removable markers, mark bottom corner sts of Front neck opening. With RS facing, using smaller needle(s), beginning at right edge of Back neck, pick up and knit 1 st for every CO st across Back neck, approximately 3 sts for every 4 rows down left Front to first marked st, making sure to pick up an even number of sts, pm, 1 st for every CO st across Front neck to second marked st, pm, and approximately 3 sts for every 4 rows up right Front to shoulder, making sure to end with an even number of sts.

Rnd 1: Begin 1x1 Rib; work to 2 sts before first neck marker, skp, work in rib, beginning with a knit st, to second neck marker, k2tog, work in rib, beginning with a knit st, to end. Repeat Rnd 1 five times, working rib pattern as established. BO all sts loosely in pattern.

Block as desired.

MAKE IT YOUR OWN

With this square-neck raglan, you can alter the depth of the neckline by simply trying on as you go and adding the center front stitches when the time feels right. If you do this, be sure to take into account the depth of the neck edging you're going to add later, plus a smidge (because for some reason, the neckline on this sweater creeps up just a little more than you think it will after you've added the edging). Add sleeve length, if you want to, as long as you have enough extra yarn on hand. You can also check your own stitch pattern books and add a different motif at the center front . . . it's up to you. Just be sure that you center the correct multiple of motif stitches on the front before you start.

ZUMA TUNIC

I remember having a beach tunic like this while I was in high school and college. It was perfect to throw on when the sun began to dip below the horizon. Worked with a wonderful mix of organic wool and cotton, this tunic is a perfect, casual, multiseason garment. Make it a smidge longer if you want to cover a bathing suit.

YOKE

Using 29"-long circ needle and MC, CO 1 (2, 2, 2, 2, 4, 6) st(s) for right Front, pm, 2 (4, 4, 4, 4, 2, 2) sts for Right Sleeve, pm, 18 (20, 20, 24, 26, 30, 32) sts for Back, 2 (4, 4, 4, 4, 2, 2) for Left Sleeve, pm, and 1 (2, 2, 2, 2, 4, 6) st(s) for left Front—24 (32, 32, 36, 38, 42, 48) sts. Purl 1 row.

Note: Yoke and neck shaping are worked at the same time; please read entire section through before beginning. Fronts will not be joined until after the Sleeves are separated and the Body has begun.

Shape Yoke (RS): Begin St st, increase 8 sts this row, then every other row 22 (23, 24, 25, 28, 28, 31) times, as

PATTERN FEATURES

Top-down raglan construction, simple shaping, stranded colorwork, picking up and knitting.

SIZES

X-Small (Small, Medium, Large, 1X-Large, 2X-Large, 3X-Large)

FINISHED MEASUREMENTS

32 (34½, 36¼, 40½, 44¾, 48, 52¼)" chest

YARN

Tunney Wool Company O-Wool Balance (50% certified organic merino wool / 50% certified organic cotton; 120 yards / 50 grams): 6 (7, 7, 8, 9, 10, 12) hanks #1000 Natural; 1 (1, 1, 1, 1, 2, 2) hank(s) #3125 Jade (A): 1 hank each #3017 Peridot (B) and #8014 Agate (C)

NEEDLES

One 29" (70 cm) long or longer circular (circ) needle size US 6 (4 mm)

One or two 24" (60 cm) long or longer circular needles or one set of five double-pointed needles (dpn) size US 6 (4 mm), as preferred, for Sleeves

One or two 24" (60 cm) long or longer circular needles or one set of five double-pointed needles size US 4 (3.5mm), as preferred, for Sleeves

Change needle size if necessary to obtain correct gauge.

NOTIONS

Stitch markers; waste yarn

GAUGE

19 sts and 28 rows = 4" in Stockinette stitch (St st), using larger needle

follows: [Knit to 1 st before marker, k1-f/b, sm, k1-f/b] 4 times, knit to end. AT THE SAME TIME, beginning on row 20 (20, 22, 22, 24, 24, 24) after CO, shape neck as follows:

Shape Neck (RS): Continuing with Yoke shaping as established, increase 1 st each neck edge this row, then every 4 rows 2 (2, 2, 3, 3, 3, 3) times, as follows: K1-f/b, work to last st, k1-f/b.

Next Row (RS): CO 5 (5, 5, 6, 7, 7, 6) sts, work to end, CO 5 (5, 5, 6, 7, 7, 6) sts. Do NOT join. Working back and forth, work even until Yoke shaping is complete—224 (240, 248, 264, 292, 296, 324) sts.

BODY

Next Row (RS): Knit across 32 (34, 35, 38, 42, 44, 48) sts of left Front, transfer next 48 (52, 54, 56, 62, 60, 66) sts to waste yarn for Left Sleeve, removing markers, CO 6 (7, 8, 10, 11, 13, 14) sts for underarm, pm for side, CO 6 (7, 8, 10, 11, 13, 14) sts for underarm, knit across 64 (68, 70, 76, 84, 88, 96) sts of Back, transfer next 48 (52, 54, 56, 62, 60, 66) sts to waste yarn for Right Sleeve, removing markers, CO 6 (7, 8, 10, 11, 13, 14) sts for underarm, pm for side, CO 6 (7, 8, 10, 11, 13, 14) sts for underarm, knit across 32 (34, 35, 38, 42, 44, 48) sts of right Front—152 (164, 172, 192, 212, 228, 248) sts. Working back and forth, work even for 13 rows.

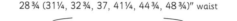

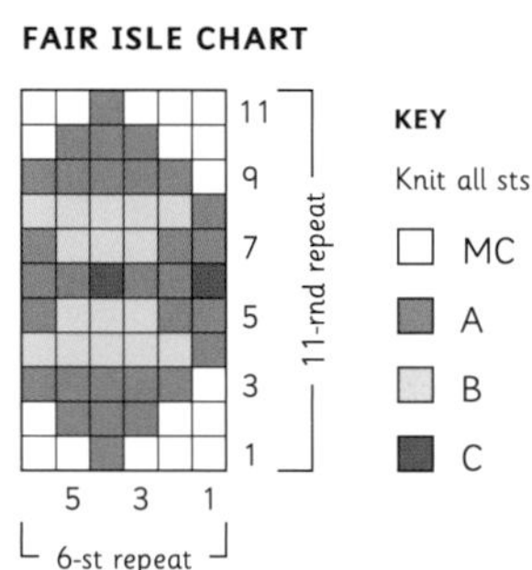

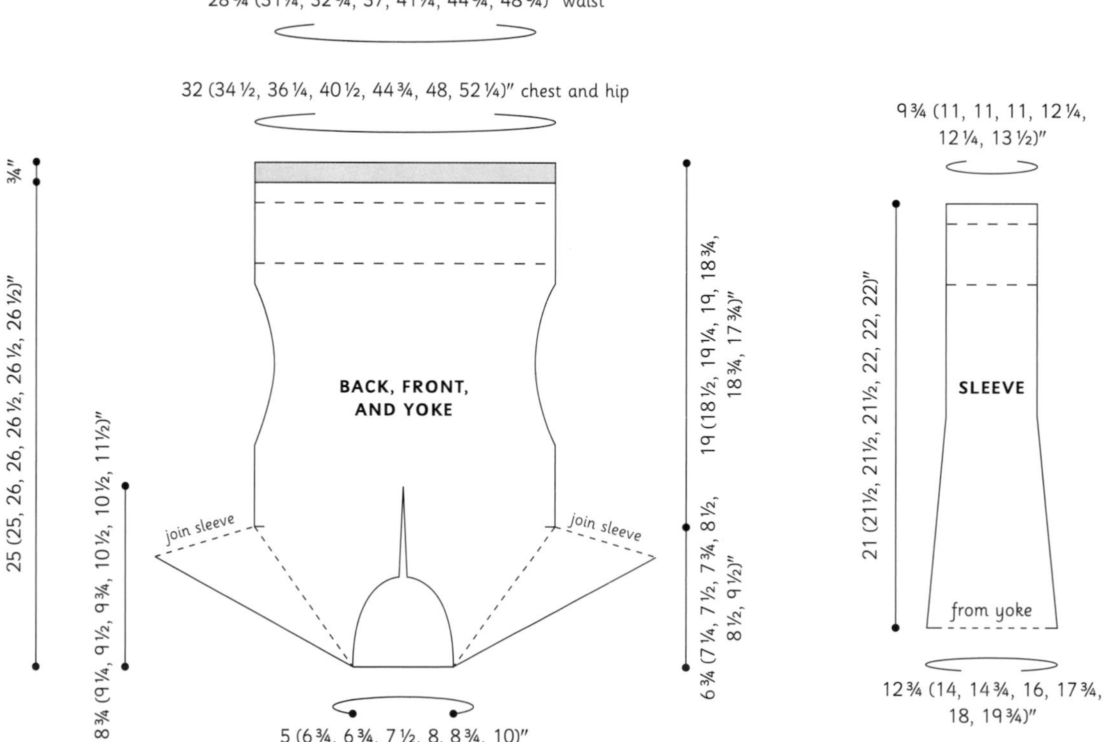

Join Fronts (RS): Join for working in the rnd, work across left Front to side marker (now beginning of rnd marker). Work even until piece measures 4¼ (4, 4¾, 4½, 4, 4, 3¼)" from underarm.

Shape Waist: Decrease 4 sts this rnd, then every 7 rnds 3 times, as follows: [K1, k2tog, knit to 3 sts before next marker, ssk, k1, sm] twice—136 (148, 156, 176, 196, 212, 232) sts remain. Work even for 13 rnds.

Shape Hip: Increase 4 sts this rnd, then every 7 rnds 3 times, as follows: [K1, m1, knit to 1 st before marker, m1, k1, sm] twice—152 (164, 172, 192, 212, 228, 248) sts. Work even until piece measures 13 (12¾, 13½, 13¼, 12¾, 12¾, 12)" from underarm, increase 4 (4, 2, 0, 4, 0, 4) sts evenly on last rnd—156 (168, 174, 192, 216, 228, 252) sts.

Next Rnd: Change to Fair Isle Pattern from Chart; work even until 2 vertical repeats of Chart have been completed. Change to MC; work even for 4 rnds.

Begin Slit: Knit to first marker, turn, removing marker, knit to next marker, turn, removing marker. Working back and forth on Front sts only, continuing in Garter st (knit every row), work even for 6 rows. BO all sts loosely knitwise. With RS facing, rejoin yarn to Back sts; knit 1 row.

Next Row (WS): K5 (edge sts, keep in Garter st), purl to last 5 sts, k5 (edge sts, keep in Garter st). Work even for 5 rows, keeping first and last 5 sts in Garter st, and remaining sts in St st. Change to Garter st across all sts; work even for 6 rows. BO all sts loosely knitwise.

SLEEVES

Note: Use your preferred method of working in the rnd when working the Sleeves (see page 23).

Transfer Sleeve sts from waste yarn to larger needle(s). With RS facing, join MC at underarm; begin St st, work to end, pick up and knit 6 (7, 8, 10, 11, 13, 14) sts from sts CO for underarm, pm for beginning of rnd, pick up and knit 6 (7, 8, 10, 11, 13, 14) sts from sts CO for underarm—60 (66, 70, 76, 84, 86, 94) sts. Join for working in the rnd; work even for 7 rnds.

Shape Sleeve: Decrease 2 sts this rnd, then every 10 (10, 8, 6, 5, 5, 5) rnds 1 (3, 1, 2, 10, 6, 2) time(s), then every 9 (9, 7, 5, 4, 4, 4) rnds 5 (3, 7, 9, 2, 7, 12) times, as follows: K1, k2tog, work to last 3 sts, ssk, k1—46 (52, 52, 52, 58, 58, 64) sts remain. Work even until piece measures 16½ (17, 17, 17, 17½, 17½, 17½)" from underarm, or to 4½" less than desired length, increase 2 sts evenly on last rnd—48 (54, 54, 54, 60, 60, 66) sts.

Next Rnd: Change to Fair Isle Pattern from Chart; work even until 2 vertical repeats of Chart have been completed. Change to MC; work even for 4 rnds. Change to Garter st (purl 1 rnd, knit 1 rnd); work even for 4 rnds. BO all sts loosely purlwise.

FINISHING

Neckband: Using 24"-long circ needle and MC, beginning at center Back neck, pick up and knit sts evenly around neck opening. Join for working in the rnd; pm for beginning of rnd. Knit 1 rnd. BO all sts loosely knitwise.

Block as desired.

MAKE IT YOUR OWN

Add a hood (see page 22) to make the tunic more California-beach style, or change the colorwork bands to personalize it even more. Just be sure that you adjust the multiple of stitches on the needles to accommodate whatever pattern you choose.

CHAPTER 5

Knitting Swaps: Tricks and Techniques for Substituting Yarn, Gauge, and Stitch Patterns

Every now and then, we all find a pattern that calls our name, yet isn't constructed the way we'd like it to be. "If only this stitch pattern were written in the round," we might say to ourselves, or "If only I could substitute a worsted-weight yarn I have in my stash for the sport weight it calls for." The good news is, very often it's possible to make these adjustments. Keep in mind that if you plan to make substitutions, you'll probably have to do things like adjust stitch counts and possibly even use a calculator. It may feel scary at first, but this mini leap could be your first step in learning how to design from scratch.

CUSTOMIZING CONSTRUCTION

In this section, I show you a few different knitting parlor tricks that will help you adapt patterns to your liking. Converting stitch patterns from flat and bottom-up to in-the-round and upside down; changing gauge; swapping out yarn; and converting a pattern that's written in pieces to in-the-round.

Converting Stitch Patterns

Working exclusively in one piece has its advantages, but along with these benefits comes certain challenges. For one thing, if you want to incorporate a stitch pattern into a garment that you plan to work in the round, you'll find that most stitch dictionaries only write patterns to be worked flat. Not only that, the stitch patterns are almost always oriented as if the knitter would work from the bottom of the garment up toward the top. Read on to find out how to convert your stitch pattern to suit the needs of your pattern construction, be it in-the-round or upside-down.

CONVERTING A STITCH PATTERN TO IN-THE-ROUND

To show you how to convert a stitch pattern to in the round, I've used the Horseshoe Print stitch pattern as an example. You'll see that it has a multiple of 10 stitches plus 1 extra stitch. That 1 stitch represents an edge stitch, or a stitch that is knit or purled to maintain or offset the pattern. When you convert a flat stitch pattern to in-the-round, the first thing you need to do is look at the rows of the pattern and the information contained within the asterisks (if the pattern is written out), or indicated by the brackets and stitch repeat information (if charted). Then, you need to remove the extra stitch(es) on one or both side(s) of the pattern.

Things can get a little tricky if the edge stitches vary in number. For example, let's say you see a "K1" before the asterisk in one right-side row and then a "K4" in the next right-side row. If you were to simply knit the stitches that appear within the asterisks, your pattern wouldn't line up correctly. Instead, take a look at the varying number of stitches that appear before the asterisk. If on the first row there is a "K1" before the asterisk, and on the second right-side row there is a "K4" before the asterisk, subtract the "K1" from the second "K4" and work only 3 knit stitches at the beginning of that next right-side round. If you are confused about where the pattern begins and ends, it may help to approach it visually. Get some graph paper and chart out a couple repeats of the pattern. Draw a line on either side of the pattern repeat and eliminate the stitches that are not needed.

Once you've removed the edge stitches, you need to convert your stitch pattern so that each row becomes a right-side round. That means, on every other round, you'll need to work "inside-out" (i.e., the knits become purls and the purls become knits). If you happen to have chosen a pattern that has slipped stitches, be aware that you may need to slip the stitches with the yarn in front instead of with the yarn in back or vice versa. Also note that all rounds in charts will now be read from right to left instead of right to left on right-side rows and left to right on wrong-side rows (as in flat knitting).

If your chosen pattern isn't symmetrical, travels in one direction only, or is offset to the left or right, you'll want to pause and rethink your wrong-side rows. They will no longer be worked from left to right, but instead, from right to left. So if you want the motif to travel in the intended direction, you not only need to change your knits to purls and purls to knits—you also need to change the wrong-side rows so that they are backwards.

Unless you're some sort of Ginger Rogers with mad skillz in photographic memory or something, I highly suggest you get yourself a pencil and some paper and write everything out, turning the wrong-side rows around as you write them. Then you can work a swatch with your revised in-the-round instructions to make sure you haven't missed anything.

FLAT TO ROUND: CONVERTING A SIMPLE LACE PATTERN

Here is the Horseshoe Lace stitch pattern that I used for the Satsuma Bolero on page 123. Since most stitch patterns start out as flat patterns, it was necessary for me to convert it so it would work in the round. As you can see, this is a simple pattern to convert. Since all the extra stitches before the asterisk were the same, I just omitted that first stitch on all rounds. Converting the wrong-side rows was simple, too, since all I had to do was change the knits to purls and the purls to knits.

Horseshoe Lace (worked flat)
(multiple of 10 sts + 1; 8-row repeat)
Row 1 (RS): K1, *yo, k3, sk2p, k3, yo, k1; repeat from * to end.
Row 2 and all WS Rows: Purl.
Row 3: K1, *k1, yo, k2, sk2p, k2, yo, k2; repeat from * to end.
Row 5: K1, *k2, yo, k1, sk2p, k1, yo, k3; repeat from * to end.
Row 7: K1, *k3, yo, sk2p, yo, k4, repeat from * to end.
Row 8: Purl.
Repeat Rows 1–8 for Horseshoe Lace (worked flat).

HORSESHOE LACE CHART
(worked flat)

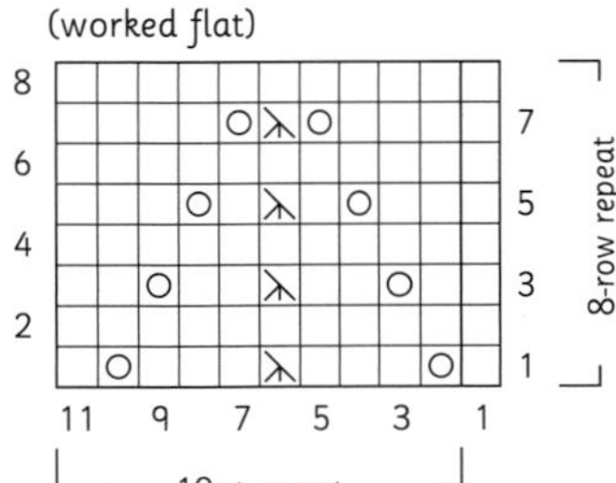

KEY

- ☐ Knit on RS, purl on WS.
- Yo
- Sk2p

HORSESHOE LACE CHART
(worked in the rnd)

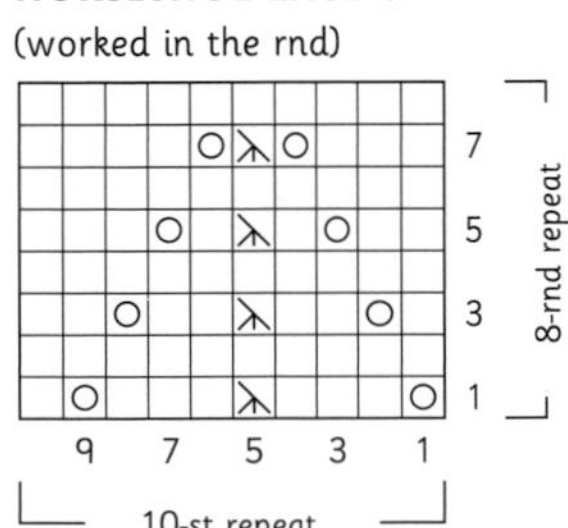

KEY

- ☐ Knit
- Yo
- Sk2p

Cheat Sheet for Converting Flat to Round

When you convert a stitch pattern from flat to in-the-round, refer to this chart to see how stitches appear on the right side and wrong side.

RIGHT SIDE	WRONG SIDE
Purl	Knit
Knit	Purl
Yo	Yo
K1-tbl	P1-tbl
K2tog	P2tog
Ssk	Ssp
P2tog	K2tog
M1 knitwise	M1 purlwise
M1 purlwise	M1 knitwise
K2tog, yo	Yo, p2tog
Ssk, yo	Yo, ssp
Wyib	Wyif
Wyif	Wyib

Horseshoe Lace (worked in-the-rnd)
(multiple of 10 sts; 8-rnd repeat)
Rnd 1: *Yo, k3, sk2p, k3, yo, k1; repeat from * to end.
Rnd 2 and all Even-Numbered Rnds: Knit.
Rnd 3: *K1, yo, k2, sk2p, k2, yo, k2; repeat from * to end.
Rnd 5: *K2, yo, k1, sk2p, k1, yo, k3; repeat from * to end.
Rnd 7: *K3, yo, sk2p, yo, k4; repeat from * to end.
Rnd 8: Knit.
Repeat Rnds 1–8 for Horseshoe Lace (worked in the round).

TURNING A STITCH PATTERN UPSIDE DOWN

Most patterns that contain simple combinations of knit and purl stitches do not need any special treatment when it comes to flipping them "upside down" in preparation for top-down knitting. Usually, you just need to get them to work in the round, if that is how you are knitting. But what do you do when you realize that the stitch pattern with leaves that travel upward in the swatch will travel downward when you knit it from the top down? First, note that not every stitch pattern or motif is a candidate for being turned upside down. There's only one way to find out if it will work—make a swatch. Make your first swatch "as is" and get to know the pattern before you attempt to reorient it. Once you have worked the swatch as it is written and examined it carefully, convert the "flat" pattern into one that is in the round (assuming you are working in the round). Then, proceed by doing one of the next two steps.

1 Write out the pattern first, as if it were bottom-up. Then, literally rewrite it from the last row to the first row. For example, in a 6-row/round stitch pattern, row/round 6 becomes the row/round 1, row/round 5 becomes row/round 2, and so on. This will turn things around so your cables or pattern run in the right direction for knitting top down.

2 Or, get out some graph paper and plot out the stitches (for in-the-round knitting) from the bottom up using conventional knitting symbols, then physically turn it upside down and study it. If you're working a lace pattern, where yarnovers and decreases are paired so that there is no change in stitch count, you will see that yarnovers remain yarnovers, and decreases continue to lean in their original direction. For cable patterns, you may need to exchange a cable that crosses in front for one that crosses in back. For example, look at the charts at right, where the traditional Staghorn Cable is flipped upside down and becomes the Reverse Staghorn Cable.

STAGHORN VEST (SEE PAGE 72) FEATURES REVERSE STAGHORN CABLE

If you are trying to flip a stitch pattern that increases or decreases from the bottom to the top, you need to convert your decreases to increases and your increases to decreases. If they lean a particular way, you'll have to work the increase in the same direction. For example, a right-leaning decrease, like a k2tog, should be turned into a right-leaning make-one. Alternatively, an ssk, which is a left-leaning decrease, should be turned into a left-leaning make-one. What about a double decrease, where 2 stitches are decreased? This is trickier and probably not the easiest to reproduce when working top-down. You could probably work an increase like a k1-f/b/f or a p1-f/b/f, but it won't look exactly the same. That isn't to say that you should not attempt to convert a stitch pattern that includes double decreases or stitches that simply do not look exactly the same when turned upside down. It's just important that should you make the attempt, that you work a swatch for yourself, and get a little crafty when it comes to mimicking the original stitches.

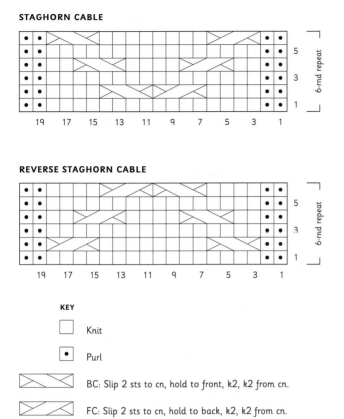

STAGHORN CABLE

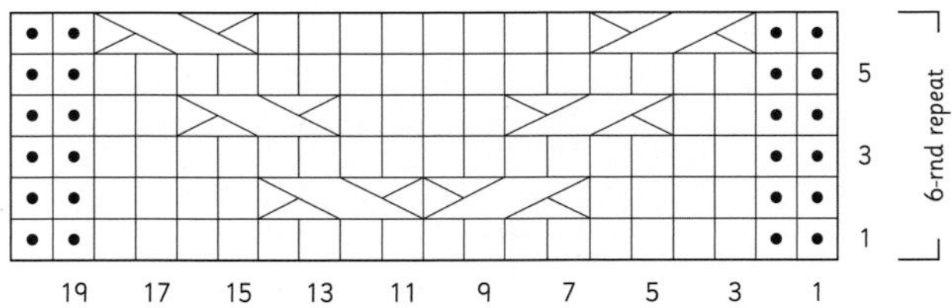

REVERSE STAGHORN CABLE

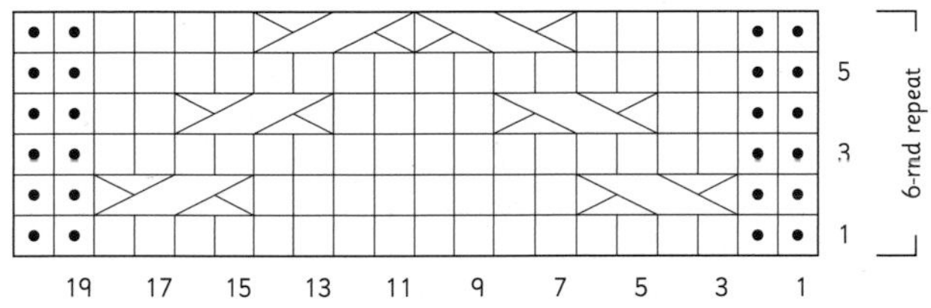

KEY

Knit

Purl

BC: Slip 2 sts to cn, hold to front, k2, k2 from cn.

FC: Slip 2 sts to cn, hold to back, k2, k2 from cn.

Converting Gauge

Have you ever come across a pattern that you really want to knit, but then realized that you don't have the correct yarn on hand? Or maybe you'd like to see the pattern worked with finer stitches for a more delicate look, or larger stitches to make the knitting go faster? The good news is, you can absolutely change your gauge and swap out one yarn for another. But be forewarned: When you substitute yarn, not only do you have to take into account gauge issues, but changing the yarn weight and fiber content can drastically impact the garment's drape. For example, look at Satsuma (shown at top on page 112) and compare it to its variation below. Even though gauge was converted, the yarn content is drastically different from the main version, which is 100 percent wool. The variation is drapey, and even though gauge was converted, the garment hangs completely differently than the original—it is as if it is a completely different pattern altogether.

Some people think it's okay to work a pattern as is if your gauge is only off by a half stitch, but there are dangers with this line of thinking. For instance, if the pattern calls for a gauge of 5 stitches and 7 rows to the inch and the yarn you select has 4 ½ stitches and 6 rows per inch, it will be off by a half stitch and one row. If the sweater you're making has a chest circumference of 40" at a gauge of 5 stitches per inch, with 200 stitches at its largest circumference, and if you happily work the pattern as written with your substituted yarn at 4 ½ stitches per inch, you'll try it on only to discover that it is way too big. Why? Take a look at the numbers: At 200 stitches, your sweater's circumference will be 44 ½" (200 ÷ 4 ½ stitches per inch = 44 ½"). That's a total of 4 ½ extra inches.

Then look at the difference in row gauge. If the pattern specifies that you work 6 rows in between three sets of waist shaping units, you will have three sets of 7 rows in that section, or 21 total rows that should equal a total of 3". Problem is, your substituted yarn will yield you 3 ½" in that section. Not only will your sweater be too big around, it'll be longer than it's supposed to be, as well. Not to mention, at that rate, you could run out of yarn!

Even though substituting yarns can be tricky, it isn't impossible. In fact, armed with a calculator and a generous swatch of the yarn you plan to use, you should do just fine.

CONVERTING STITCH GAUGE

1 Make up a swatch that is at least 4" x 4".

2 Carefully measure how many stitches your swatch yields to the inch (measure across all 4" and divide the number of stitches by 4 to get your result).

3 Compare your swatch to the gauge called for in the pattern and determine if you need to add or subtract stitches. For example, the pattern calls for 24 stitches over 4" but your swatch has 20 stitches. That means you will require fewer stitches than what the pattern calls for.

SATSUMA (SEE PAGE 123) MADE WITH 100% WOOL YARN AND WORKED AT A LARGER GAUGE

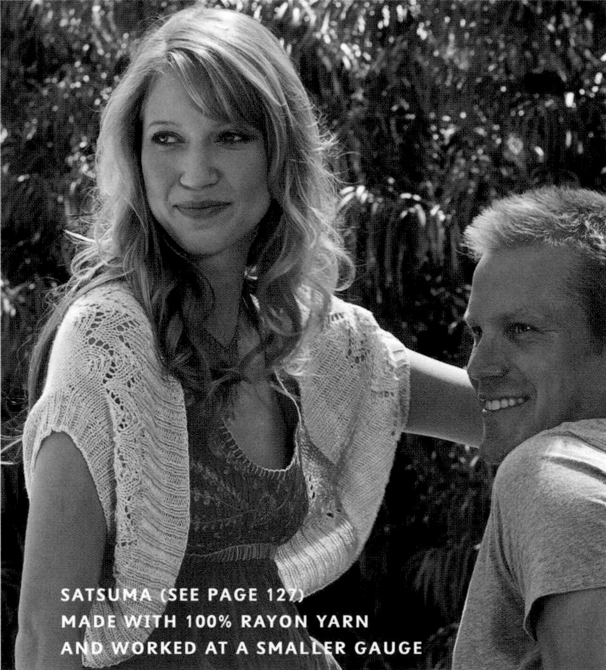

SATSUMA (SEE PAGE 127) MADE WITH 100% RAYON YARN AND WORKED AT A SMALLER GAUGE

4 Beginning with the gauge, divide the called-for number (24) by your number (20) to get the required factor of stitches (24 ÷ 20 = 1.2), which means that when you cast on stitches, you take the called-for number and divide it by 1.2 to find out the number of stitches you will cast on instead. For example, let's say the cast on number is 100 sts and it will yield an approximately 16 ½" wide fabric, but your gauge will require fewer sts to make that same width of fabric. So, what you do is take the cast on number of 100 and divide it by 1.2 (100 ÷ 1.2 = 83.3). Round the number down to 83 stitches (adjusting if necessary to accommodate stitch pattern multiples) and cast on that number to get the required width of fabric (83 stitches ÷ 5 stitches per inch = 16.6"). *Note: Whenever you regauge a pattern, it is imperative that you check your math against the schematic whenever possible. There might be times when you want to round the number of stitches up or down.*

CONVERTING ROW GAUGE

1 Using your generous swatch as your guide, carefully measure how many rows your swatch yields to the inch.

2 *Note: Knitting patterns may express length in both rows and inches within the same pattern.* Say the pattern expects a row gauge of 8 rows per inch and your swatch measures 7 rows per inch, and the instructions for the body of the sweater direct you to knit a section to 10". You can figure out how many rows you need to knit at your own gauge of 7 rows per inch by multiplying the directed length (10") by your gauge of 7 rows per inch: 7 rows x 10" = 70 rows.

3 If the pattern expresses a knit-to length in terms of rows (for example, the pattern says: "Work even for 82 rows"), you will need to calculate the length required by the pattern first, before moving on. If the row gauge in the pattern is 8 rows per inch and the pattern wants you to knit 82 rows, you will divide 82 rows by the required 8 rows per inch: 82 rows ÷ 8 rows per inch = 10 ¼". Using this length, you have the choice to simply knit until your own section measures 10 ¼" OR you may convert these 10 ¼" into your own personal number of rows. Do this by multiplying the number of inches by your number of rows per inch: 10 ¼" x 7 rows per inch = 71.75 rows, or 72 rows, if you round it up.

OTHER CONSIDERATIONS WHEN CONVERTING GAUGE

If you are changing the gauge of a garment more than one or two stitches or rows per inch, you will have to consider how it will affect the overall look. The following sections cover a few things that you should keep in the back of your mind as you convert the gauge of your pattern.

Working Motifs with Substituted Yarn

If you have chosen a project that contains motifs, such as panels of lace, cables, or ribs, a new gauge will affect the overall look. If you choose a yarn with a smaller gauge, your motif will be narrower and take up less space; if you choose a yarn with a larger gauge, your motif will be wider and take up more space. Once you've noted how your new yarn will affect your motif, you may need to make adjustments to the pattern so that you get the look you want.

Motifs usually require a particular stitch count beyond the simple "even" or "odd" number of stitches that are required. For instance, in the case of the Horseshoe Lace that was chosen for Satsuma on page 123, it calls for a multiple of 10 stitches. Consider, however, if you have a beginning gauge of 20 stitches to 4". That means you'll have two repeats of the pattern for every 4" of knitting. If you switch to a much finer gauge, say 24 stitches to four inches, you'll get approximately two and a half motifs in the same number of inches. What this means is that, in areas where the motif is placed, you might have to make your garment slightly larger or smaller to accommodate the correct repeat of stitches. This is especially important if the adjusted area lands in places where you must have a good fit, like hips or sleeves, or across the chest. When you are forced to adjust stitch counts up or down to accommodate a motif, just grab your calculator to determine if the new circumference you've calculated will still fit your body.

In the case of a centered panel of ribs, lace or cables, it's always a good idea to swatch with your substituted yarn and measure its width to see if you want to add more pattern repeats. Obviously, when going up in gauge, you might decide you want to subtract a repeat, if the pattern calls for more than one repeat. If the pattern calls for just one repeat, you may wish to consider using a motif that will require fewer stitches.

Adjusting Shaping with Substituted Yarn

When it comes to shaping, if your row gauge is off by just one row, it can alter the look and fit of the piece. Usually, when a pattern calls for waist shaping, the shaping increments occur at a fixed set of rows/rounds. *Note: This information applies equally whether you are working circularly in rounds, or back and forth in rows, but for the sake of clarity, we will just refer to "rows," rather than "rows/rounds."* If you just went ahead and followed the pattern as written, your decreases and increases would not be spaced according to the pattern or the schematic. You have a couple of choices in this situation. You could recalculate the instructions completely, or you could take the following easier route, coupled with trying on as you go.

When your pattern calls for decreases or increases that occur every nth row for a particular shaping section in the pattern, find out how many rows the portion of shaping covers. To do this, read the pattern and make note of the number of rows in which the entire section of shaping (both waist and hip) occurs. For example, say the waist shaping section (decreases) reads as follows: "Decrease 4 sts this row, then every 8 rows 3 times, as follows: [K1, k2tog, work to 3 sts before marker, ssk, k1, sm] twice." This means you will first do 1 row of decreases, work 7 rows even, repeat the decrease row, then repeat the last 8 rows 2 more times. That is a total of 25 rows (the first shaping row + 8 rows multiplied by 3 total sets of 8 rows, or 1 + [8 x 3] = 25 rows).

Now that you know the waist shaping requires 25 rows, read further into the pattern to see if there is a section of straight knitting (for example, "Work even for 7 rows.") before the hip shaping (an increase section) occurs. For the hip shaping, the pattern will read as follows: "Increase 4 sts this row, then every rows 3 times, as follows: [K1, m1, work to 1 st before marker, m1, k1, sm] twice." Just like the waist shaping, the section of increases will require 25 rows, PLUS the 7 rows where you work even. So, in this particular pattern, there are 25 initial rows of shaping, 7 rows of even knitting and 25 rows of final shaping, or 57 total rows of shaping.

Since the original pattern in our example calls for a row gauge of 8 rows per inch, the next thing you need to do is calculate the length in which the shaping occurs. Do this by dividing the number of 57 total rows by the 8 rows per inch: 57 rows ÷ 8 rows per inch = 7″. This means that the pattern is directing you to achieve your shaping within a 7″ span.

Since with your yarn and your needles you have a row gauge of 7 stitches per inch, if you were to work those 57 rows at your personal gauge, you'd end up working a section of shaping that spans about 8¼″: That's 1¼″ longer than the pattern intends. To fix this, you will have to figure out the frequency in which you do your waist and hip shaping according to your new gauge. First, based on what we learned before, that the waist shaping (decreases) occurred over 25 rows, or 3″ (25 rows ÷ 8 rows per inch = 3 inches), refigure how many rows you will have with your new gauge or, 3″ x 7 rows per inch = 21 rows, or 4 rows less than you would have had in the pattern. In this example, what you would do is subtract the first shaping row from the desired number of rows, then divide the resulting number of rows (20) by the remaining number of shaping increments (3), 20 rows ÷ 3 increments = 6⅔. So, instead of following the pattern, simply work your initial decrease row, then work 3 more decrease rows every 7 rows. Note that when you are working back and forth, if you prefer to work decreases and increases only on right-side rows, you will have to adjust the shaping accordingly. In our example, you might choose to work all the decreases every 6 or 8 rows, or some every 6 and some every 8 rows. You could also adjust the number of even rows between the decrease and increase sections, so that you still maintain the desired overall number of rows in the shaping section.

Now you can probably see where you are going: Work 6 rows even instead of the called-for 7 rows, and then repeat your frequency in the increase portion of the shaping as before: increase on the next row, and then increase again every 7 rows 3 times, which will give you a total of 50 rows of shaping that will yield you nearly the same number of inches as in the original pattern. (50 rows ÷ 7 rows per inch = 7″ of knitting.)

Converting Bottom-Up Pieced Patterns to In-the-Round or One-Piece

It happens to a lot of us: We spot a pattern we'd really like to knit, but it's worked bottom-up and in pieces and we much prefer to work in-the-round. There are some garments, like heavy coats, that make sense to work in pieces, since the seams add structure (especially in larger sizes). Plus, if you are working a large, heavy garment all in one piece, it would eventually weigh quite a lot and wouldn't be easy to manipulate in your lap. That said, if you come across a pattern that is worked from the bottom-up and in pieces and feel it would be better to make it in the round in one piece, it's possible to convert most, if not all, of the pattern. Follow these steps to convert a bottom-up pieced pullover or cardigan to in-the-round.

1 Read through the "back" section of the pattern (this part usually comes first) and note how many stitches you're meant to cast on. For a pullover pattern, the back and fronts are very likely the same. For a cardigan pattern, you will have a back and two fronts. If the fronts are symmetrical, each front will have the same number of stitches to be cast on. Take a look at these pieces and determine if there is an extra stitch on either side. Some designers add an extra stitch on either side of the back and on the "underarm" sides of the fronts for seaming. If your pattern does this, and let me tell you, you won't always know it unless the pattern calls the extra stitch the "edge stitch" or "selvage stitch" or something of that nature, you will need to omit them. For a pullover, to calculate your initial cast-on: (back stitches + front stitches) – edge stitches = _____. Check to make sure this number of stitches works with the multiple of stitches of any ribbing or other stitch patterns that appear in the garment, and if the multiple isn't correct, add or subtract stitches from your fronts and back to arrive at the correct even multiple.

2 If you are converting a pullover and it has a stitch pattern, you will need to convert it to in-the-round (see page 108) meaning that every round will be a right-side round. Stitch patterns on cardigans won't be affected since you will still be working back and forth—you'll just be omitting the side seams. If a pattern needs to be centered, you will need to omit any extra edge stitches when you cast on so that the pattern stays centered.

3 Take note of the direction you will be working. If the original pattern is a bottom-up pullover, you'll work one side first, place a marker, then work the other side next, then place a marker and join in the round. *Keep in mind that every round is a right-side round.* If you are working a cardigan, things change a little bit. Instead of working in rounds, you'll be working a front, placing a marker, working the entire back, placing a marker, working the other front, and turning and working back and forth, up toward the neck. As you work the garment, whether it be a pullover or cardigan, add new markers for shaping that occurs in areas other than the sides. When you are directed to do waist shaping, it will look best if you offset the shaping increments by 1 stitch on either side of the marker. In other words, when you are directed to do a decrease, work to 3 stitches before the marker, knit 2 together, and knit the stitch before the marker. The same holds true for any other decrease, such as a slip, slip, knit (ssk).

4 When you reach the armhole shaping, simply place the front(s) on a holder or waste yarn and work the back separately and back and forth up to the shoulders, then put the back on a holder or waste yarn. Work the front section as written, up to the shoulders. Place the back shoulder stitches onto a spare needle and work a Three-Needle BO for a nice, seamless shoulder (see Special Techniques page 153).

5 For sleeves, you can follow the original pattern, working the sleeves flat and seaming them in later. Or you can join them in the round (remembering to omit extra edge stitches) and work them up to about an inch before the sleeve cap shaping starts. Then, change to working flat for that inch. Work the shaping as written, then set in your sleeve and seam it. If you want your pullover to be completely seamless, ignore the pattern and add your own Afterthought Sleeves (see page 23), working from the top down. If your pattern has sleeves that are a unique shape and you are an experienced knitter, it probably won't be too difficult to reverse-engineer them so they look similar in your in-the-round, top-down "afterthought" conversion. Just be sure to take note of any special stitch patterns that may need to be flipped upside down or converted to in-the-round.

SIZES

X-Small (Small, Medium, Large, 1X-Large, 2X-Large, 3X-Large)

FINISHED MEASUREMENTS

32 (35, 37¾, 42¼, 45¾, 50¼, 52¼)" chest, unbuttoned

YARN

Elsebeth Lavold Silky Wool (45% wool / 35% silk / 20% nylon; 192 yards / 50 grams): 4 (5, 5, 6, 6, 7, 7) hanks #54 Coffee Bean Brown

NEEDLES

One 32" (80 cm) long or longer circular (circ) needle size US 6 (4 mm)

One or two 24" (60 cm) long or longer circular needles or one set of five double-pointed needles (dpn) size US 6 (4 mm), as preferred, for Sleeves

One pair straight needles size US 4 (3.5 mm) (optional, for button cover)

Change needle size if necessary to obtain correct gauge.

NOTIONS

Stitch markers; waste yarn; one ¼" button

GAUGE

22 sts and 28 rows = 4" (10 cm) in Stockinette stitch (St st)

EYELET CARDIGAN

Most round yoke sweaters are worked from the bottom up, but this one is worked from the top down so you'll be able to try on as you go for a perfect fit under the arms. If you want to substitute a different eyelet pattern than the one shown here, just be sure you keep track of the multiple of stitches as you make increases down the yoke so you can accommodate your new pattern. Want to create your own round yoke sweater from scratch with yarn from your stash? See page 146 for guidelines.

PATTERN FEATURES
Top-down round-yoke construction, simple stitch pattern, simple shaping, picking up and knitting.

STITCH PATTERN

Eyelet Stitch (worked flat)
(multiple of 4 sts)
Row (RS) 1: K4, *[yo] twice, k4; repeat from * to end—2 sts increased.
Row 2: P2, *p2tog, p1, k1, p2tog; repeat from * to last 2 sts, p2—2 sts decreased.
Row 3: K2, yo, *k4, [yo] twice; repeat from * to last 6 sts, k4, yo, k2—4 sts increased.
Row 4: P3, *[p2tog] twice, p1, k1; repeat from * to last 7 sts, [p2tog] twice, p3—4 sts decreased.
Repeat Rows 1–4 for Eyelet Stitch.

YOKE

Note: After the initial CO, use Backward Loop CO for any other COs in this pattern (see Special Techniques, page 152).

Using 32"-long circ needle, CO 84 (92, 96, 100, 108, 112, 120) sts.

Next Row (WS): K6, pm, knit to last 6 sts, pm, knit to end. Work even in Garter st (knit every row) for 6 rows.

Buttonhole Row (RS): Work to last marker, sm, k1, BO 2 sts, work to end. Work even for 1 row, CO 2 sts over BO sts, work to end.

Shape Back Neck

Note: Back neck is shaped using Short Rows (see Special Techniques, page 156). Hide wraps as you come to them.

Row 1 (RS): K50 (55, 58, 60, 65, 68, 73) sts, wrp-t.

Row 2: K16 (18, 20, 20, 22, 24, 26) sts, wrp-t.

Rows 3–8: Knit to 3 (3, 3, 3, 6, 6, 6) sts past wrapped st of row before last row worked, wrp-t.

Next Row (RS): Knit to end, hiding remaining wrap as you come to it. Knit 1 row.

Shape Yoke

Increase Row 1 (RS): Knit, increase 12 (12, 12, 12, 16, 16, 16) sts evenly spaced between markers, working increases as k1-f/b—96 (104, 108, 112, 124, 128, 136) sts. Knit 1 row.

Next Row (RS): Knit to marker, sm, work Eyelet st to next marker, sm, knit to end. Work even for 7 rows, working Garter st on the first and last 6 sts, and Eyelet st on the sts between markers. Knit 2 rows.

Increase Row 2 (RS): Knit, increase 20 (20, 24, 24, 24, 24, 24) sts evenly spaced between markers, working increases as k1-f/b—116 (124, 132, 136, 148, 152, 160) sts. Knit 3 rows.

Next Row (RS): Work 4 rows, working Garter st on the first and last 6 sts, and Eyelet st between markers. Knit 2 rows.

Increase Row 3 (RS): Knit, increase 32 (32, 36, 36, 36, 36, 36) sts evenly spaced between markers, working increases as k1-f/b—148 (156, 168, 172, 184, 188, 196) sts. Knit 3 rows.

Next Row (RS): Work 4 rows, working Garter st on the first and last 6 sts, and Eyelet st between markers. Knit 2 rows.

Increase Row 4 (RS): Knit, increase 36 (36, 40, 40, 40, 40, 40) sts evenly spaced between markers, working increases as k1-f/b—184 (192, 208, 212, 224, 228, 236) sts. Knit 3 rows.

Next Row (RS): Work 4 rows, working Garter st on the first and last 6 sts, and Eyelet st between markers. Knit 2 rows.

Increase Row 5 (RS): Knit, increase 48 (52, 56, 60, 40, 48, 52) sts evenly spaced between markers, working increases as k1-f/b—232 (244, 264, 272, 264, 276, 288) sts. Knit 3 rows.

Next Row (RS): Work 8 (8, 8, 8, 4, 4, 4) rows, working Garter st on the first and last 6 sts, and Eyelet st between markers. Knit 2 rows.

Increase Row 6 (RS): Knit, increase 60 (64, 68, 68, 48, 52, 56) sts evenly spaced between markers, working increases as k1-f/b—292 (308, 332, 340, 312, 328, 344) sts. Knit 3 rows.

Sizes – (–, –, –, 1X-Large, 2X-Large, 3X-Large) Only:

Next Row (RS): Work 8 rows, working Garter st on the first and last 6 sts, and Eyelet st between markers. Knit 2 rows.

Increase Row 7 (RS): Knit, increase – (–, –, –, 24, 28, 32) sts— – (–, –, –, 336, 356, 376) sts. Knit 3 rows.

All Sizes:

Next Row (RS): Continuing to work Garter st on first and last 6 sts, change to St st between markers; work even until piece measures 8 (8½, 8½, 9, 9½, 10, 10½)" from the beginning, measuring along Front edge, and ending with a WS row. *Note: Measurements made from the center Back neck will be ¾" longer due to short-row neck shaping.*

BODY

Join Back and Fronts (RS): K42 (43, 47, 50, 51, 55, 58) sts, transfer next 62 (68, 72, 70, 66, 68, 72) sts to waste yarn for Left Sleeve, CO 2 (5, 5, 8, 12, 14, 14) sts for underarm, pm for side, CO 2 (5, 5, 8, 12, 14, 14) sts for underarm, k84 (86, 94, 100, 102, 110, 116) sts for Back, transfer next 62 (68, 72, 70, 66, 68, 72) sts to waste yarn for Right Sleeve, CO 2 (5, 5, 8, 12, 14, 14) sts for underarm, pm for side, CO 2 (5, 5, 8, 12, 14, 14) sts for underarm, knit to end—176 (192, 208, 232, 252, 276, 288) sts. Continuing to work Garter st on first and last 6 sts, and St st between markers, work even until piece measures 1 (½, 1, ½, 1, 1½, 1)" from underarm, ending with a WS row.

Shape Waist (RS): Decrease 4 sts this row, then every 8 rows 3 times, as follows: [Work to 3 sts before side marker, ssk, k1, sm, k1, k2tog] twice, work to end—160 (176, 192, 216, 236, 260, 272) sts remain. Work even for 7 rows.

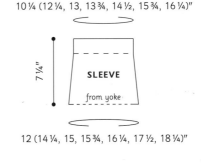

29 (32, 35, 39¼, 43, 47¼, 49½)" waist

32 (35, 37¾, 42¼, 45¾, 50¼, 52¼)" chest and hip

19 (19, 20, 20, 22, 22, 22)"

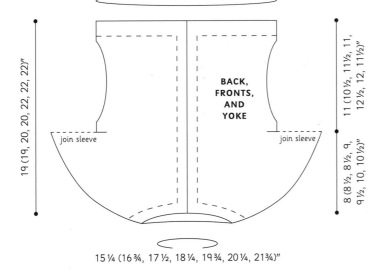

BACK, FRONTS, AND YOKE

join sleeve

join sleeve

11 (10½, 11½, 11, 12½, 12, 11½)"

8 (8½, 8½, 9, 9½, 10, 10½)"

15¼ (16¾, 17½, 18¼, 19¾, 20¼, 21¾)"

10¼ (12¼, 13, 13¾, 14½, 15¾, 16¼)"

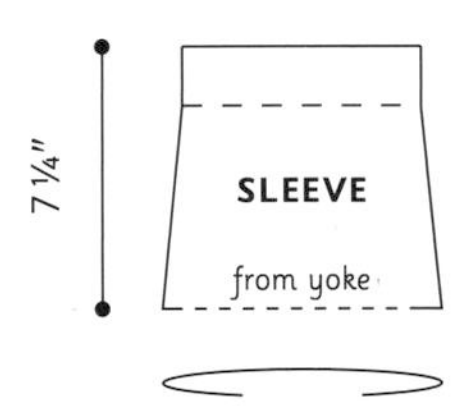

12 (14¼, 15, 15¾, 16¼, 17½, 18¼)"

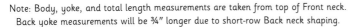

Note: Body, yoke, and total length measurements are taken from top of Front neck. Back yoke measurements will be ¾" longer due to short-row Back neck shaping.

Shape Hips (RS): Increase 4 sts this row, then every 8 rows 3 times, as follows: [Work to 1 st before side marker, m1, k1, sm, k1, m1] twice, work to end—176 (192, 208, 232, 252, 276, 288) sts. Work even until piece measures 9½ (9, 10, 9½, 11, 10½, 10)" from underarm, ending with a RS row. Change to Garter st; work even for 14 rows. BO all sts loosely knitwise.

SLEEVES

Note: Use your preferred method of working in the rnd when working the Sleeves (see page 23).

Transfer 62 (68, 72, 70, 66, 68, 72) Sleeve sts to needle(s). With RS facing, rejoin yarn at center of underarm, pick up and knit 2 (5, 5, 8, 12, 14, 14) sts from sts CO for underarm, pm for beginning of rnd, knit to end, pick up and knit 2 (5, 5, 8, 12, 14, 14) sts from sts CO for underarm—66 (78, 82, 86, 90, 96, 100) sts. Join for working in the rnd. Work even for 7 rnds.

Shape Sleeve: Decrease 2 sts this rnd, then every 8 rnds 4 times, as follows: K1, k2tog, work to last 3 sts, ssk, k1—56 (68, 72, 76, 80, 86, 90) sts remain. *Note: If you wish a longer sleeve, work even to 1½" from desired length.* Change to Garter stitch (purl 1 rnd, knit 1 rnd); work even for 14 rnds. BO all sts loosely purlwise.

FINISHING

Sew button to Left Front, centered in Garter st bands.

Block as desired.

MAKE IT YOUR OWN

Whenever there is a stitch pattern or a motif, know that you have an opportunity to switch it up, personalize it, or even omit it if you want. To swap a motif, take a swatch to check that your gauge won't change. Then check to make sure that your stitch counts will have the correct multiple of stitches at each key point in the sweater so that you can incorporate your new stitch pattern or motif. No one will be the wiser. A word of warning, however: Because you are knitting from the top down, any stitch pattern, cable, or motif that you find in a stitch pattern book will be worked upside down. See page 110 for tips on dealing with this.

SATSUMA BOLERO

This bolero has an interesting construction that begins with a rectangular Back section. Stitches are then picked up all around the rectangle's edges to create the border. The two versions shown here are a lesson in how different fibers can affect the drape of a garment. The wool one at left is in a worsted gauge with short-ish sleeves, while the variation on page 126 is in a finer gauge rayon yarn and practically sleeveless. If you'd like to read more on how to alter the gauge of any existing pattern, see page 111.

PATTERN FEATURES

On-the-fly unique construction, provisional cast-on, simple stitch pattern, ribbing.

SIZES

X-Small (Small, Medium, Large, 1X-Large, 2X-Large, 3X-Large)

FINISHED MEASUREMENTS

13¾ (14¾, 15½, 17, 17¾, 18¼, 19)" across top Back

YARN

Lorna's Laces Shepherd Worsted (100% superwash wool; 225 yards / 100 grams): 2 (3, 3, 3, 4, 4, 4) hanks #509 Satsuma

NEEDLES

One 32" (80 cm) long or longer circular (circ) needle size US 7 (4.5 mm)

One 32" (80 cm) long or longer circular needle size US 6 (4 mm)

One or two 24" (60 cm) long or longer circular needles or one set of five double-pointed needles (dpn) size US 7 (4.5 mm), as preferred, for Sleeves

One or two 24" (60 cm) long or longer circular needles or one set of five double-pointed needles size US 6 (4 mm), as preferred, for Sleeves

Change needle size if necessary to obtain correct gauge.

NOTIONS

Waste yarn, stitch markers

GAUGE

18 sts and 24 rows = 4" (10 cm) in Stockinette stitch (St st), using larger needle

STITCH PATTERNS

Horseshoe Lace

(multiple of 10 sts; 8-rnd repeat)

Rnd 1: *Yo, k3, sk2p, k3, yo, k1; repeat from * to end.

Rnd 2 and all Even-Numbered Rnds: Knit.

Rnd 3: *K1, yo, k2, sk2p, k2, yo, k2; repeat from * to end.

Rnd 5: *K2, yo, k1, sk2p, k1, yo, k3; repeat from * to end.

Rnd 7: *K3, yo, sk2p, yo, k4; repeat from * to end.

Rnd 8: Knit.

Repeat Rnds 1–8 for Horseshoe Lace.

2x2 Rib

(multiple of 4 sts; 1-rnd repeat)

All Rnds: *K2, p2; repeat from * to end.

NOTE

This Shrug begins with a shaped Back. The oval Edging Band that forms the fronts, Back neck, and Back waist is worked from the top and bottom of the Back stitches, with stitches cast on at either side edge of the Back to form armholes. The Edging Band is worked in the round, with short-row shaping in the ribbing section. The Sleeves are picked up from the sides of the Back and the cast-on stitches of the Edging Band and worked in the round to the bottom edge.

HORSESHOE LACE CHART

(worked in the rnd)

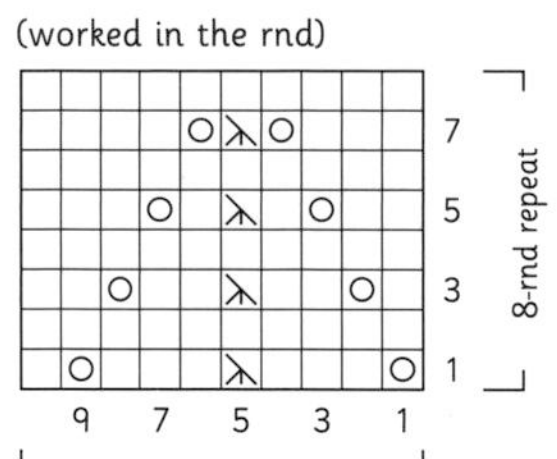

KEY

Knit

Yo

Sk2p

BACK

Note: After the Provisional CO, use Backward Loop CO for any other COs in this pattern (see Special Techniques, page 152). Back is worked from the bottom up.

Using larger 32"-long circ needle, waste yarn and Provisional CO, CO 68 (72, 82, 90, 104, 114, 118) sts. (RS) Change to working yarn. Begin St st; work even for 4 rows.

Shape Back (RS): Decrease 1 st each side this row, then every other row 2 (2, 5, 6, 11, 15, 15) times, as follows: K2, ssk, work to last 4 sts, k2tog, k2—62 (66, 70, 76, 80, 82, 86) sts remain. Work even until piece measures 3½ (4½, 5, 5½, 6, 6½, 6½)" from the beginning, ending with a WS row. Leave sts on needle.

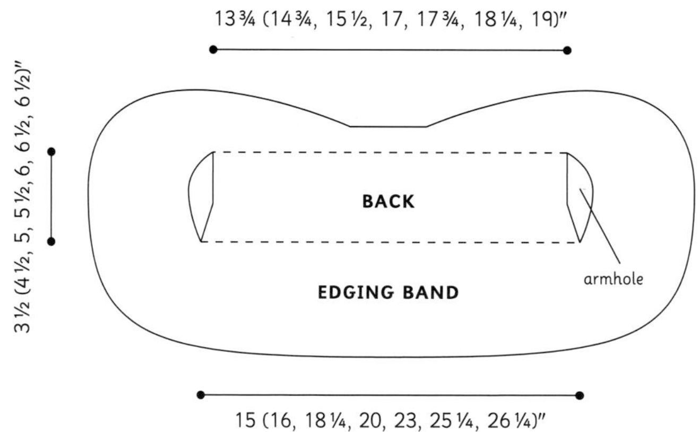

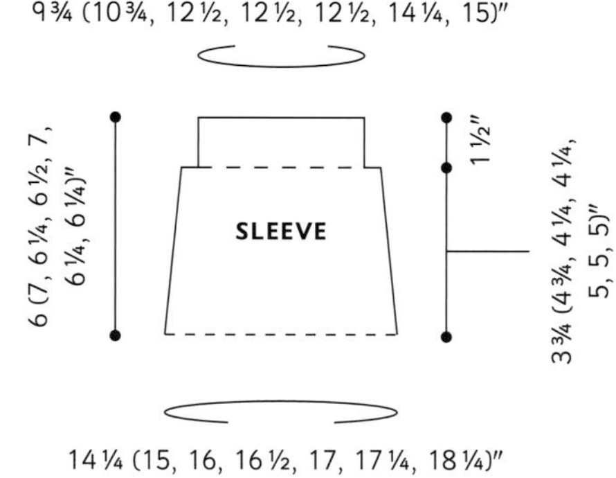

EDGING BAND

With RS facing, carefully unravel Provisional CO and place sts on spare needle. K31 (33, 35, 38, 40, 41, 43) Back sts, pm for beginning of rnd (this marks center Back neck), k31 (33, 35, 38, 40, 41, 43), CO 48 (50, 52, 52, 52, 52, 54) sts for left armhole, knit across 68 (72, 82, 90, 104, 114, 118) sts from Provisional CO, CO 48 (50, 52, 52, 52, 52, 54) sts for right armhole, knit to end—226 (238, 256, 270, 288, 300, 312) sts.

Next Rnd: Continuing in St st work even for 8 (10, 13, 16, 19, 22, 25) rnds, decrease 6 (8, 6, 0, 8, 0, 2) sts evenly on last rnd—220 (230, 250, 270, 280, 300, 310) sts remain.

Next Rnd: Change to Horseshoe Lace; work even until 2 vertical repeats of pattern have been completed, decrease 0 (2, 2, 2, 0, 0, 2) sts evenly on last rnd of pattern—220 (228, 248, 268, 280, 300, 308) sts remain.

Next Rnd: Change to smaller 32"-long circ needle and 2x2 Rib, placing markers 26 (29, 30, 29, 31, 32, 34) sts to either side of beginning of rnd marker.

Shape Band

Note: Band will be shaped using Short Rows (see Special Techniques, page 156). Hide wraps as you come to them.

Row 1 (RS): Working back and forth and continuing in 2x2 Rib, work to second marker, sm, wrp-t.

Row 2: Work to next marker, sm, wrp-t.

Row 3: Work to wrapped st of row before last row worked, work wrapped st, work 2 sts, wrp-t.

Repeat Row 3 until 7 (7, 8, 7, 6, 7, 6) sts remain on either side of beginning of rnd marker.

Next Rnd (RS): Change to working in the rnd, hiding remaining wrap as you come to it, and removing all markers except beginning of rnd marker. Work even for 3 rnds. BO all sts loosely in pattern.

SLEEVES

Lay piece flat with RS up and Back neck facing away from you; mark bottom center of each armhole. With RS facing, and beginning at marker, pick up and knit 64 (68, 72, 74, 76, 78, 82) sts around armhole opening. Join for working in the rnd; pm for beginning of rnd. Begin St st; work even for 1 (1, 5, 3, 3, 5, 5) rnd(s).

Shape Sleeve: Decrease 2 sts this rnd, then every 3 (3, 3, 3, 3, 5, 3) rnds 6 (8, 5, 6, 7, 3, 5) times, as follows: K1, k2tog, work to last 3 sts, ssk, k1—50 (50, 60, 60, 60, 70, 70) sts remain. Work even until piece measures 3¾ (4¾, 4¼, 4¼, 5, 5, 5)" from underarm.

Next Rnd: Change to Horseshoe Lace; work even for 8 rnds, decrease 6 (2, 4, 4, 4, 6, 2) sts evenly on last rnd—44 (48, 56, 56, 56, 64, 68) sts remain. Change to smaller needles and 2x2 Rib; work even for 10 rnds. BO all sts loosely in pattern.

FINISHING

Block as desired.

MAKE IT YOUR OWN

Substitute another yarn without fear by following the instructions on page 111. If you're a beginner and don't want to follow a complicated stitch pattern, work Stockinette stitch for the whole piece. The sleeves can be lengthened as you see fit. I think belled sleeves would look fabulous.

The white variation at left is worked at a smaller gauge than the original pattern, and the new gauge has MORE stitches per inch than the base pattern. The original Satsuma has 18 stitches per 4" and we required 24 stitches per 4" for the variation you see here. In order to convert gauge, a factor was found by dividing the OLD gauge by the NEW gauge (18 ÷ 24 = .75). Since the new gauge has MORE stitches than the old gauge, more stitches will be required in order to make the correct width or circumference of the fabric. Whenever there is a cast-on amount or other added or subtracted stitches in the pattern, we will divide the old number by the stitch gauge factor (.75 in this case) to arrive at the correct number. In the beginning, Satsuma calls for a cast-on number of 72 for the size small. So, 72 ÷ .75 = 96 stitches, which will yield approximately the same width of fabric. Note, whenever you regauge a pattern, it is imperative that you check your math against the schematic whenever possible. There might be times when you want to round up or round down the number of stitches.

Instead of adding sleeves as described in the main pattern, approximately 2 out of 3 stitches are picked up around the armhole circumference, starting with the center underarm, in a multiple of 4. Then, 2x2 rib is worked in the round for approximately 2" and bound off in pattern. Since there are more stitches to the inch in the variation, that means there will be more stitches in between markers for the short-row shaping that forms the ribbing around the Body, so you will have to work more short rows to complete the shaping. This is not a problem, but rather a welcome situation because just two repeats of the Horseshoe Lace are worked in the variation and the Body needs a little more depth.

The variation was worked in size small with just one hank (550 yards) of Blue Heron Rayon Metallic in Polar Bear—Silver. Read about estimating yarn requirements on page 15.

SIZES

X-Small (Small, Medium, Large, 1X-Large, 2X-Large, 3X-Large)

FINISHED MEASUREMENTS

33½ (37, 38½, 43, 46½, 51, 54½)" chest

YARN

Shibui Knits Merino Kid (55% kid mohair / 45% merino; 218 yards / 100 grams): 4 (5, 5, 5, 6, 6, 7) hanks Wasabi

NEEDLES

One 32" (80 cm) long or longer circular (circ) needle size US 7 (4.5 mm)

One 32" (80 cm) long or longer circular needle size US 6 (4.25 mm)

One or two 16" (40 cm) long or longer circular needle(s) or one set of five double-pointed needles (dpn) size US 7 (4.5 mm), as preferred, for Sleeves

One or two 16" (40 cm) long or longer circular needle(s) or one set of five double-pointed needles size US 6 (4.25 mm), as preferred, for Sleeves

Change needle size if necessary to obtain correct gauge.

NOTIONS

Waste yarn; removable marker; stitch markers

GAUGE

20 sts and 24 rows = 4" (10 cm) in Stockinette stitch (St st), using larger needles

WASABI

What I love best about this sweater is its drop-shoulder construction. You cast on at mid-back and work up toward the shoulder, then after stitches are bound off for the neck, you work down the front to the underarms and join in the round to work toward the hem. An extra bonus is that the sleeves are knit with the wrong side facing, so when you turn everything right side out, you have some nifty Reverse Stockinette stitch with hardly any effort at all. You say you enjoy purling? Then, by all means, work the Reverse Stockinette stitch parts of the sweater with the right sides facing you.

PATTERN FEATURES

Top-down construction, provisional cast-on, picking up and knitting, ribbing.

STITCH PATTERNS

2x2 Rib (worked flat)

(multiple of 4 sts; 2-row repeat)

Row 1 (RS): K3, *p2, k2; repeat from * to last st, k1.

Row 2: P3, *k2, p2; repeat from * to last st, p1.

Repeat Rows 1 and 2 for 2x2 Rib.

2x2 Rib (worked in the rnd)

(multiple of 4 sts; 1-rnd repeat)

All Rnds: *K2, p2; repeat from * to end.

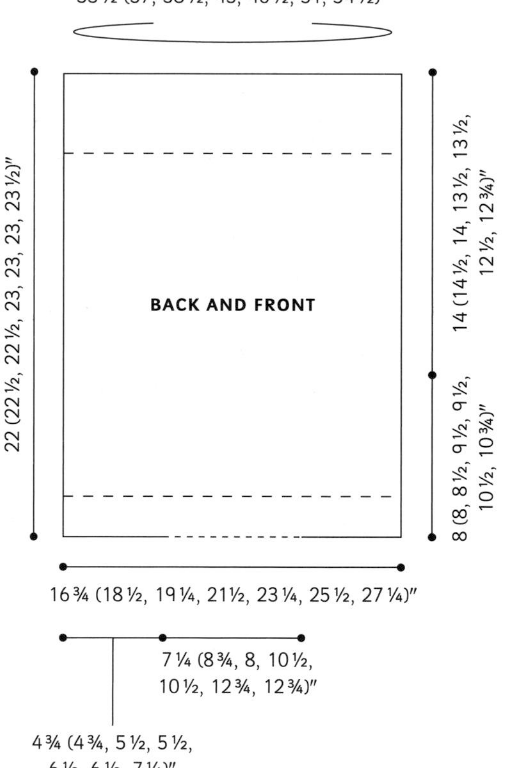

NOTE

The Body of this piece is begun at the center Back, worked over the shoulders to the center Front, then joined at the armholes and worked in the round down to the bottom edge.

The yarn used in this pattern, once blocked, provides a flat ribbing that does not pull in. If you are substituting yarn, make a test swatch to be sure that the ribbing will lie flat; otherwise, it will draw in and make a "blouson" effect. It may be necessary to use the larger needles with substituted yarn so that the ribbing does not pull in.

YOKE BACK AND FRONT

Note: After the initial Provisional CO, use Backward Loop CO for any other COs in this pattern (see Special Techniques, page 152).

Using larger 32" circ needle, waste yarn and Provisional CO, CO 84 (92, 96, 108, 116, 128, 136) sts. Change to working yarn; begin St st. Work even until piece measures 6 (6, 6 ½, 7 ½, 7 ½, 8 ½, 8 ¾)" from the beginning, ending with a WS row. Change to smaller needle and 2x2 Rib (worked flat); work even for 2", ending with a WS row. Place removable marker at beginning of row to mark RS and top of shoulder.

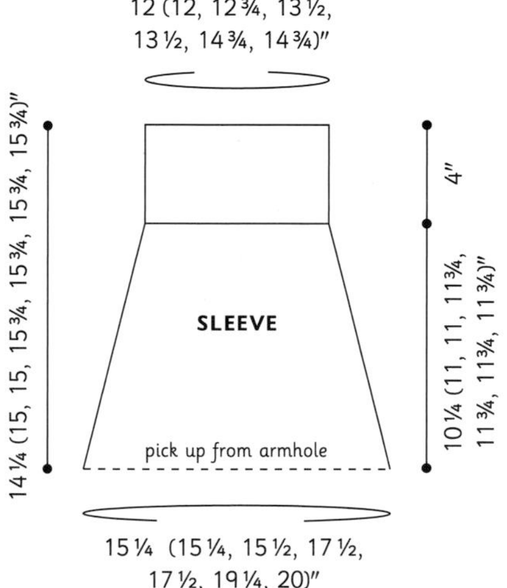

Shape Neck (RS): Work 24 (24, 28, 28, 32, 32, 36) sts, BO 36 (44, 40, 52, 52, 64, 64) center sts loosely in pattern, work to end.

Next Row (WS): Work to BO sts, CO 36 (44, 40, 52, 52, 64, 64) sts, work to end. Work even in 2x2 Rib for 2", ending with a WS row. Change to St st; work even until piece measures 6 (6, 6½, 7½, 7½, 8½, 8¾)" from top of shoulder, ending with a WS row.

BODY

Join Back and Front (RS): With RS facing, carefully unravel Provisional CO and place Back sts on left-hand end of circ needle. Work across Front sts, then across Back sts—168 (184, 192, 216, 232, 256, 272) sts. Join for working in the rnd; pm for beginning of rnd. Continuing in St st, work even until piece measures 10 (10½, 10, 9½, 9½, 8½, 8¾)" from underarm. Change to smaller needle and 2x2 Rib (worked in the rnd); work even for 4". BO all sts loosely in pattern.

SLEEVES

Note: Use your preferred method of working in the rnd when working the Sleeves (see page 23).

Turn piece inside out so that WS is facing; this will create pick-up ridges on the RS. Using larger needle(s), beginning at bottom center of underarm, pick up and knit 76 (76, 78, 88, 88, 96, 100) sts evenly around armhole. Join for working in the rnd; pm for beginning of rnd. Begin St st; work even for 6 (5, 7, 2, 2, 5, 4) rnds.

Shape Sleeve: Decrease 2 sts this rnd, then every 7 (8, 9, 7, 7, 6, 5) rnds 7 (7, 6, 9, 9, 10, 12) times, as follows: K1, k2tog, knit to last 3 sts, ssk, k1—60 (60, 64, 68, 68, 74, 74) sts remain. Work even until piece measures 10¼ (11, 11, 11¾, 11¾, 11¾, 11¾)" from pick-up rnd. BO all sts loosely. Do not cut yarn.

SLEEVE CUFF

With WS facing, using smaller needle(s) and attached yarn, pick up and knit 60 (60, 64, 68, 68, 72, 72) sts from BO edge. Join for working in the rnd; pm for beginning of rnd. Begin 2x2 Rib (worked in the rnd); work even for 4". BO all sts loosely in pattern.

FINISHING

Turn piece RS out.

Block as desired.

MAKE IT YOUR OWN

It would be fun to add a ribbed neckline edging about 3" long so it splays out "just so." To do this, pick up stitches around the neckline and work the edging of your choice.

If you don't want exposed seams, or want Stockinette stitch on your sleeves, simply pick up the stitches with the right side facing instead, and knit in the round down to the cuff, working the sleeve shaping as instructed. If you want something even less fitted, so you can layer, work at least one size up.

SIZES

Youth (Women's Small/Medium, Women's Large/Men's Small)

FINISHED MEASUREMENTS

16¼ (20, 21¾)" brim, unstretched

Note: The brim is fairly stretchy; it is recommended to work a size that is 2" smaller than desired circumference.

YARN

Nashua Handknits Creative Focus Silk (100% silk; 120 yards / 50 grams): 2 balls #CFS.0847 Yolk

NEEDLES

One 16" (40 cm) long circular (circ) needle size US 5 (4 mm)

One set of five double-pointed needles (dpn) size US 5 (4 mm)

Change needle size if necessary to obtain correct gauge.

NOTIONS

Stitch markers; 1 yard fine clear elastic (optional)

GAUGE

22 sts and 28 rows = 4" in Gumdrop Pattern

22 sts and 30 rows = 4" in Stockinette stitch (St st)

LEMON DROP

In Southern California, it's simply too warm too often to get any real mileage out of a hat. (Though, oddly, I do see many folks at the gym who wear knit beanies while they're working out and obviously don't mind having a sweaty head.) Me? If I'm going to wear a hat, it's for pure fun and fashion. I tend to choose blends of yarn that contain cotton or silk and avoid hats made of wool. But if you're looking for a cap like this that'll keep you warm, simply substitute a woolen yarn in the same weight.

PATTERN FEATURES
Bottom-up construction, simple stitch pattern, simple shaping.

STITCH PATTERN

Gumdrop Pattern
(multiple of 5 sts; 4-rnd repeat)
Rnds 1–3: *P2, k3; repeat from * to end.
Rnd 4: *P2, yo, sk2p, yo; repeat from * to end.
Repeat Rnds 1–4 for pattern.

BRIM

Using circ needle, CO 90 (110, 120) sts. Join for working in the rnd, being careful not to twist sts; pm for beginning of rnd. Begin Garter st (purl 1 rnd, knit 1 rnd); work even for 1½", ending with a purl rnd. Knit 1 rnd, increase 20 sts (using m1 increase) evenly spaced—110 (130, 140) sts.

Rnds 1–4: Work Gumdrop Pattern.

Rnds 5–6: Work Garter st, beginning with a purl rnd.

Repeat Rnds 1–6 until piece measures approximately 5½ (7, 7½)" from the beginning, ending with Rnd 4 of Gumdrop Pattern. Purl 1 rnd.

Shape Crown

Note: Change to dpns when necessary for number of sts on needles.

Decrease Rnd 1: *K2tog; k3; repeat from * to end—88 (104, 112) sts remain. Purl 1 rnd, decrease 3 (4, 2) sts evenly spaced—85 (100, 110) sts remain.

Work Rnds 1–4 of Gumdrop Pattern. Purl 1 rnd.

Decrease Rnd 2: Repeat Decrease Rnd 1—68 (80, 88) sts remain. Purl 1 rnd, decrease 3 (0, 3) sts evenly spaced—65 (80, 85) sts remain.

Work Rnds 1–4 of Gumdrop Pattern. Purl 1 rnd.

Decrease Rnd 3: Repeat Decrease Rnd 1—52 (64, 68) sts remain. Purl 1 rnd, decrease 2 (4, 3) sts evenly spaced—50 (60, 65) sts remain.

Work Rnds 1–3 of Gumdrop Pattern.

Decrease Rnd 4: *P2tog, yo, sk2p; repeat from * to end—30 (36, 39) sts remain. Purl 1 rnd.

Decrease Rnd 5: *K2tog, k1; repeat from * to end—20 (24, 26) sts remain. Purl 1 rnd, decrease 4 (4, 6) sts evenly spaced—16 (20, 20) sts remain.

Decrease Rnd 6: *K2tog; repeat from * to end—8 (10, 10) sts remain. Cut yarn, leaving an 8" tail. Thread tail through remaining sts, pull tight, and fasten off.

FINISHING

Block as desired. Thread elastic through Brim (optional).

MAKE IT YOUR OWN

For more slouch, work the cap portion an extra inch or two before beginning decreases; for less slouch, work one or two fewer inches before beginning decreases. Substitute woolen yarn in the same weight for a warmer hat.

CANDY

Throw Candy over a sweet summer dress and you'll have just a bit of warmth without covering up your style. Worked in one piece in a fuzzy yarn with jaunty tucks along one side, this is a fun knit with an angelic halo.

SIZES

X-Small (Small, Medium, Large)

FINISHED MEASUREMENTS

34¼ (36½, 36½, 38¼)" circumference at upper edge

38¼ (41, 44½, 49)" circumference at lower edge

YARN

Rowan Kidsilk Haze (70% super kid mohair / 30% silk; 229 yards / 25 grams): 2 balls #626 Putty

NEEDLES

One 29" (70 cm) long or longer circular (circ) needle size US 5 (3.75 mm)

One 29" (70 cm) long or longer circular needle size US 6 (4 mm)

Change needle size if necessary to obtain correct gauge.

NOTIONS

Stitch markers

GAUGE

18 sts and 24 rows = 4" in Stockinette stitch (St st), using larger needles

CAPELET

Using smaller needle, CO 154 (164, 164, 172) sts. Join for working in the rnd, being careful not to twist sts; pm for beginning of rnd. Begin 2x2 Rib; work even until piece measures 3½" from the beginning. Change to St st (knit every rnd); work even for 6 rnds.

Shape Capelet

Increase Rnd 1: *K24 (26, 12, 10), m1, k1; repeat from * to last 4 (2, 8, 7) sts, knit to end—160 (170, 176, 187) sts. Work even in St st for 2 rnds.

Tuck Rnd 1: K58 (62, 64, 70) sts, T2/R2, T2/R4, T32/R6, T2/R4, T2/R2, knit to end. Work even for 4 rnds.

PATTERN FEATURES
Knit on the fly and in the round, simple ribbing, optional tucks.

ABBREVIATION

Tx/Rx: Tuck x sts, working x rows below st on left-hand needle. The tucks in this pattern are a series of picked-up sts. Each tuck st is picked up from the WS and worked together with the next st on the left-hand needle. In each series of tucks, which are 2 to 64 sts long, with varying row depths, you will begin by picking up a specified st from a specified number of rows below the next st on the needle, and working it with the next st; this is considered one tuck st. Then, continuing with that same tuck, you will pick up 1 or more additional sts, one at a time, and work them together with a st on the needle. The tucks are worked in 5 series; when you are finished with the first series of tucks, you will continue working a different number of tuck sts over a different number of rows below the needle, so that when all the tucks are completed, they will appear to be curved. To create a tuck st, rotate the work forward so that the WS is showing, pick up the purl bump of the st in the specified row below the next st on the left-hand needle with the right-hand needle and place it onto the left-hand needle, knit the lifted st together with the next st. Repeat this process for the specified number of tuck sts. So for instance, if it says T2/R4, you tuck 2 sts (one at a time), working into the st 4 rows below the next st on the left-hand needle.

STITCH PATTERN

2x2 Rib
(multiple of 4 sts; 1-rnd repeat)
All Rnds: *K2, p2; repeat from * to end.

Increase Rnd 2: *K25 (27, 13, 10), m1, k1; repeat from * to last 4 (2, 8, 11) sts, knit to end—166 (176, 188, 203) sts. Work even in St st for 4 rnds.

Tuck **Rnd 2:** K54 (58, 60, 66) sts, T2/R2, T2/R4, T40/R6, T2/R4, T2/R2, knit to end. Work even in St st for 4 rnds.

Increase Rnd 3: *K26 (28, 14, 10), m1, k1; repeat from * to last 4 (2, 8, 16) sts—172 (182, 200, 220) sts. Work even in St st for 8 rnds.

Tuck Rnd 3: K50 (54, 56, 62) sts, T2/R2, T2/R4, T48/R6, T2/R4, T2/R2, knit to end. Work even in St st for 8 rnds.

Tuck Rnd 4: K46 (50, 52, 58) sts, T2/R2, T2/R4, T56/R6, T2/R4, T2/R2, knit to end. Work even in St st for 8 rnds.

Tuck Rnd 5: K42 (46, 48, 54) sts, T2/R2, T2/R4, T64/R6, T2/R4, T2/R2, knit to end. Work even in St st for 2 rnds, increase 0 (2, 0, 0) sts evenly on last rnd—172 (184, 200, 220) sts.

Change to smaller needles and 2x2 Rib; work even for 3½". BO all sts loosely in pattern.

FINISHING

Block as desired.

MAKE IT YOUR OWN

For a totally different drape, work Candy with a sport-weight linen. Cast on fewer stitches to make a more fitted wrap. If you omit the tucks, you'll have a more straightforward-looking shoulder cover. Or add length for an off-the-shoulder poncho. If you do that, just be sure you don't use a dense, heavy yarn, or else it will fall off your shoulders—a light and airy mohair would work great.

YARN

Pagewood Farms Alyeska (80% merino wool / 10% cashmere /10% nylon; 360 yards / 4 ounces): 1 hank #32 Forest Camo

NEEDLES

One 16″ (40 cm) long circular (circ) needle size US 2 (2.75mm)

Change needle size if necessary to obtain correct gauge.

NOTIONS

Stitch markers

GAUGE

32 sts and 38 rnds = 4″ (10 cm) in Stockinette stitch (St st)

MANZANITA BERET

The best part of knitting a beret top down is that you can try it on as you go and get the perfect amount of "slouch." To make the beret slouchier than the one shown here, just knit a couple of extra inches before you work the brim.

PATTERN FEATURES
Top-down construction, simple shaping, ribbing

STITCH PATTERN

1x1 Rib
(multiple of 2 sts; 1-rnd repeat)
All Rnds: *K1, p1; repeat from * to end.

NOTE

This Beret is worked from the Crown down to the Brim.

CROWN

Using CO of your choice or Provisional CO (see Special Techniques, page 154), CO 6 sts onto one dpn, leaving 8″ tail.

Rnd 1: *K1-f/b; repeat from * to end—12 sts. Divide sts onto three dpns. Join for working in the rnd; pm for beginning of rnd.

Rnd 2: Knit.

Rnd 3: *K1, k1-f/b; repeat from * to end—18 sts.

Rnd 4: Knit, placing markers after every third st (6 markers, including beginning of rnd marker). *Note: You may wish to use a different color to mark the beginning of the rnd.*

Shape Crown

Rnd 1: [K1-f/b (or m1-r if you prefer), work to 1 st before next marker, k1-f/b (or m1-r if you prefer), sm] 6 times.

Rnd 2: Knit.

Repeat Rnds 1 and 2 until there are 45 sts between markers, or 270 sts total.

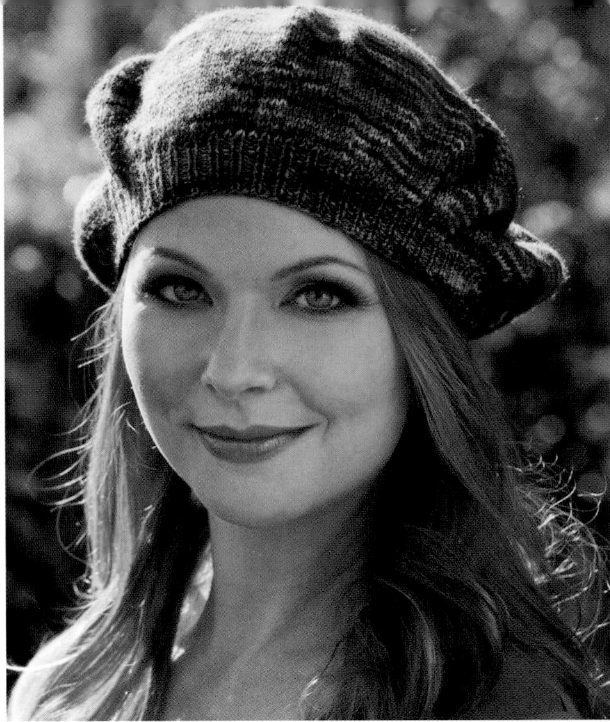

BRIM

Work even until Beret measures 7 ½″ from the beginning.

Shape Brim

Next Rnd: *K2tog; repeat from * to end—135 sts remain. Change to 1x1 Rib, decrease 1 st on first rnd—134 sts remain. Work even for 1½″ or to desired depth. BO all sts in pattern.

FINISHING

Thread CO tail through CO sts or place provisional sts onto 3 dpns and thread tail through live sts. Pull tight and fasten off. Block as desired.

MAKE IT YOUR OWN

Make a top-down beanie like the boy's slouch version using the beret pattern. Since this yarn has a gauge of 8 stitches per inch, simply cast on 8 stitches and knit into the front and back of each stitch for 1 round (16 stitches). Then, divide the stitches onto three dpns, place a marker, and join in the round. On the next round, *K1, k1-f/b; repeat from * to end—24 stitches. Knit one round and then place markers after every third stitch, making sure that you place a unique marker for the beginning of the round. You will place 8 markers instead of 6 as in the beret pattern. Then, all you do is continue working in rounds, increasing 1 stitch after each marker on every other round until you have enough stitches to achieve your desired circumference. In this case, the youth's head circumference was 21", so I worked until there were 168 stitches total (21 stitches in each section). After that, I knit to a length of 8" and then worked 2x2 Rib for another 2". This beanie required 2 hanks of Koigu KPM (100% merino; 175 yards / 50 grams) in color #2236, using size US 2 (2.75 mm) needles.

If you want to make the Pom-Pom Beanie, you'll work it the same way as the boy's slouch beanie described above, but instead of working the entire beanie in Stockinette stitch, work increases in columns between rows of garter stitch. To get started, follow the steps above until you have 24 stitches and have placed 8 markers. After that:

Rnd 1: *K1-f/b, k2, sm; repeat from * to end—32 sts.

Rnd 2: Knit.

Rnd 3: *K1-f/b, k3, sm; repeat from * to end—40 sts.

Rnd 4 and all Even-Numbered Rnds: *K2, purl to 2 sts before marker, k2, sm; repeat from * to end.

Rnds 5, 7, and 9: *K2, m1, knit to marker, sm; repeat from * to end—64 sts after Rnd 9.

Rnd 10: Repeat Rnd 4.

Then continue in this manner, increasing after the second stitch in each section on every odd-numbered round and working every even-numbered round as for Round 4, until there are 10 stitches between markers, or 80 stitches total for a 20" beanie to fit a youth or a woman's small, ending with an odd-numbered round. To shape the brim, work Round 4 and then knit 1 round. Repeat these 2 rounds until the piece measures 6" from the beginning, or to desired depth not including the Garter stitch edging. Change to Garter stitch (purl 1 rnd, knit 1 rnd) for 7 rounds and then bind off all stitches knitwise. The pom-pom was created using a 3 ½" Susan Bates Easy-Wrap Pom Pon maker and attached to the top of the cap after the stitches were picked up at the crown and cinched. The Pom-Pom Beanie required 2 hanks of Mirasol Sulka Yarn (60% merino wool / 20% alpaca / 20% silk; 55 yards / 50 grams): #201 Rose Pink. This Beanie was worked at a Stockinette stitch gauge of 16 stitches = 4" (10 cm), using size US 10 (6 mm) needles.

CHAPTER 6

Starting from Scratch

If the patterns in this book just aren't enough, why not make your very own design without a pattern? In this chapter, you'll find a couple of formulas for starting from scratch—just make sure that you keep the end in mind as you plot your fabulous creations, and check (and recheck) your progress as you knit.

Here are a couple top-down "recipes" for adventurous knitters and budding designers. Just take a few measurements, grab a calculator, and get going.

Top-Down Round-Yoke Sweater Formula

Round Yoke sweaters are usually knit from the bottom up. This is a great way to create a round yoke sweater and there's a lot of instruction out there on how to do this. But if you want to knit a top-down yoked sweater that you can try on as you go and design yourself, this formula will show you how. You can work either a pullover or a cardigan using this formula; a pullover is worked in the round, and a cardigan is worked back and forth with wrong-side and right-side rows.

A top-down round-yoke sweater construction isn't that much different from a top-down raglan sweater. The difference is that, as you work down toward the underarms, the increases are scattered in each row or round instead of placed at the sleeve joins (as you would do with a raglan). Unlike a raglan sweater—where your sleeves are created as you work the yoke—you will have to make plans for your sleeves before you get started, so that you'll have enough stitches to set aside for the sleeves, minus extra stitches you will add to the underarms later.

1 To get started, determine the following measurements:

a) Desired neck opening = _______"

b) Desired chest circumference, including any ease = _______"

c) Desired upper arm circumference, including any ease = _______"

d) Desired yoke depth (from collarbone to underarm) = _______"

Note: If you're making a cardigan and adding front bands after you finish the sweater, make an allowance for them. If the bands will overlap, subtract the width of one band from your total; if they will not overlap, subtract the width of both bands. If you plan on knitting them as you go, the bands will be included in the total width, but make sure you account for any difference in stitch gauge between the body pattern and the band pattern. In this example, there will not be front bands.

2 Make a gauge swatch, in your desired yarn, of any and all stitch patterns to be used in the piece. Make it large enough so that you can measure 4" worth of both stitches and rows, then determine your stitch and row gauge per inch.

3 When working a top-down yoked sweater, you need to plan ahead to make sure that, when all is said and done, you have the perfect number of stitches at the yoke to give you the fit you want. After you cast on for your neck, you'll work down toward your underarms, increasing as you go, so that your finished yoke will accommodate your desired custom body and sleeves. As you work this formula, pay attention to the small percentages of stitches that are subtracted from your "goal" total stitches for the body and the sleeve portions. The reason these percentages are subtracted is because you will later cast on or pick up and knit these same stitches that were initially "subtracted" at the underarm portions of the body so your custom yoked sweater flows perfectly under, over, and around your chest and arms when everything is complete.

To calculate the number of goal stitches you'll need before separating, multiply your stitch gauge by the first 3 measurements obtained in Step 1; this will tell you how many stitches you will need for the neck opening, the chest minus 16% that you will cast on at the underarms (8% at each underarm), and each sleeve minus approximately 8% that you will cast on at each underarm. Round these stitch counts to whole numbers.

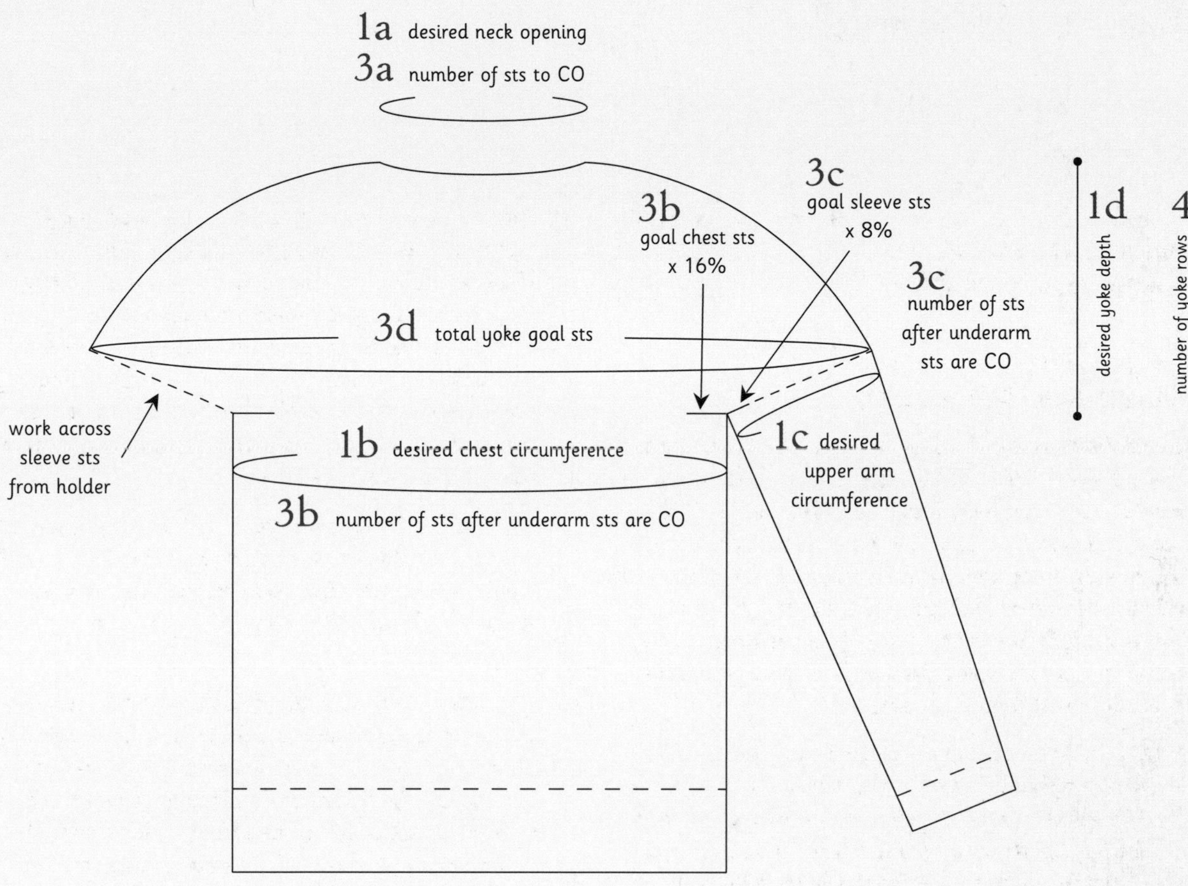

Don't forget to make adjustments for the front bands if necessary (see Step 1). In this example we will have:

a) The neck opening: X neck opening inches x _____ stitches per inch = _____ stitches to cast on.

b) The chest: X chest inches x _____ stitches per inch = _____ chest stitches; chest stitches x 16% = _____ underarm stitches; chest stitches – underarm stitches = _____ goal chest stitches before separating.

c) The upper arm circumference (upper sleeve): X upper arm inches x _____ stitches per inch = _____ sleeve stitches; sleeve stitches x 8% = _____ underarm stitches. (Round your number to something close to half of the 16%, above. It doesn't matter if this number doesn't match the number in b.) Sleeve stitches – underarm stitches = _____ goal sleeve stitches before separating.

d) Add your chest goal (the last number in b) and both your upper sleeves together (the last number in c) for your Total Yoke Goal before separating: _____.

e) Number of stitches to increase: Total Yoke Goal – initial neck cast-on = number of stitches to increase: _____.

4 Multiply your row gauge by the depth of the yoke obtained in Step 1 to determine how many rows it will take to give you the length of yoke you want. Round this to a whole number; make it an even number if you are working back and forth in rows. This calculation will tell you how many rows you'll have to do your increases. *Note: This information applies equally whether you are working circularly in rounds, or back and forth in rows, but for the sake of clarity, we will just refer to "rows," rather than "rows/rounds."*

5 Now that you've got all the stitch and row counts determined, here's a complication to consider—stitch pattern repeats. If you are working in Stockinette stitch, you don't need to worry about them. But if you are working in any stitch pattern—even those that have only 2 stitches—you will have to make sure that you have enough stitches at the neck opening and end of the yoke shaping to accommodate the pattern. And to make it even more challenging, you want to make sure that the stitch pattern multiple also works once you've added the underarm stitches to the body and sleeves. That said, it's always okay to cheat a bit and increase or decrease a stitch or two at the underarm to get to the required multiple.

6 Now that you have determined how many stitches you need at the beginning and end of the yoke (before separating the body and sleeves), and have adjusted those stitch counts to account for your stitch pattern, you need to take a look at the number of stitches you already determined so that you get from Point A (neck cast-on) to Point B (Step 3e). Divide the number of stitches to be increased by the number of increase rows that you want to work. This will give you the initial number of stitches to increase on each increase row. BUT, both the number of increase rows, and the number of increases per row, will need to be tweaked to make the yoke fit well and work with your chosen stitch pattern or motif. Read on.

7 Now that you know how many stitches you need to increase overall to get to the proper number of stitches and yoke rows, and you have an idea of how many increase rows you want to work, it's time to make some adjustments based on how many rows are in the stitch pattern or motif you will be using. Most round yoke sweaters work anywhere from 4 to 7 increase rows from cast-on to the end of the yoke. The larger the number of rows in your stitch pattern or motif (or the larger the stitch gauge), the fewer opportunities you are likely to have to work increases.

First determine how many increase rows you want to work to get to the number of stitches you need, making sure that the number you choose will work with the number of rows in your stitch pattern or motif. Your first increase row should be about 3" below the neckband, and the last should be about 1" before the end of the yoke. Subtract 4" (3 + 1) from the total yoke depth to find out how many inches you have left for the remaining increase rows, then multiply the resulting number by the row gauge. Divide that number by the remaining number of increase rows (your original number, less the first and last increase rows), rounding it down to a whole number (an even number if you're working back and forth), to find out how often you have to work an increase row. If you find that won't work with your stitch pattern or motif, try adjusting the number of increase rows that you work, until the numbers work out. You don't have to have exactly the same number of rows between increases.

Note: When working a sweater from the top down, increases (like a "make-one") lift the bar between stitches. Consequently, if there is a different color on the row above it, the color will be revealed on the row below and the overall design might be marred. If you do want to include colorwork in bands while working the sweater from the top down, you need to time your increases so they don't fall where there might be color changes.

8 Now that you know how many increase rows you're going to work, divide that number into the total number of stitches you have to increase between cast-on and the end of the yoke, to get the initial number of stitches to increase on each increase row. To make the yoke fit well, you don't want to increase the same number of stitches in each increase row. You want to consider the slope of the increases as you work down to the underarm. For a natural slope, you will want to work the smallest increment of increases first—about 3" below your neckband—and incrementally increase the number of new stitches on your next increase row as you work downward. (See Eyelet Cardigan on page 116 for an example of how the succession of increases can work.)

You'll want to start out with a small percentage of the total number of increased stitches, like maybe 10 or 15 percent on the first few increase rows, and then work your way up on each increase row; the final set of increases should include about 30 percent of the total planned number. Try on as you go, leaving the largest increase row just about shoulder height or just below it. At the end of the yoke, the increases spread out over several increase rows should add up to 100 percent of the total number of stitches you needed to add.

All of that being said, know that there isn't—and shouldn't be, as far as I'm concerned—a hard and fast rule of percentages when it comes to the progression of increased stitches on any given increase row. If you try on as you go, you will know what to do and can make decisions as you knit.

9 Once you have added all of your yoke increases and the yoke depth is what you want it to be, it's time to separate the body from the sleeves. Now refer back to your earlier calculations (Step 3 b and c) that included determining how many stitches you would cast on for each underarm. When you separate these sections, you will cast on these stitches (or the adjusted numbers you have chosen to make your stitch pattern multiples work) so you will have the correct number of stitches to reach your goal chest and sleeve circumferences.

Before you separate the body and sleeves, make sure you know how many of your yoke stitches will be set aside for the sleeves, and how many will remain for the body. This last number will be referred to below as the "yoke body stitches," as opposed to the "goal body stitches" that you will have after casting on for the underarms.

To separate body and sleeves for a cardigan, first make sure you are working on a right-side row. Work approximately one-quarter of the total number of yoke body stitches (for the first front; you may adjust the number of front stitches to accommodate planned front bands), place the correct number of sleeve stitches on waste yarn, cast on the determined number of underarm stitches using the Backward Loop CO (see Special Techniques, page 152), placing a marker at the halfway point if you plan on working body shaping, continue across one-half of the total number of yoke body stitches (back), then place the correct number of sleeve stitches onto waste yarn and repeat the cast-on that you did for the other underarm, placing another marker at the halfway point for body shaping, and work to the end. Continue in rows with a wrong side and a right side, adding shaping alongside each marker, if desired, add some edging at the hem, and bind off.

For a yoke pullover, instead of working one-quarter of the total body stitches before separating the first sleeve, like you would with a cardigan, work one-half. Separate your sleeve and cast on for the underarms, placing a marker as for the cardigan; work the other half of the total yoke body stitches and then separate your next sleeve and place your marker at the center of the next set of cast-on stitches for your other underarm. This last marker needs to be unique as it will denote the beginning of each round. Continue working the body in rounds down to the hem, adding waist shaping, if desired.

To create the sleeves, simply place the stitches on the needle(s) (for your preferred method of working the sleeves in the round, page 23). Rejoin the yarn and work to the end, pick up and knit the number of stitches you calculated in Step 3c from the underarm stitches you cast on for the body. Your preplanned number of stitches to be picked up (or added to) your sleeves may not match the stitches you cast on for the Body, but that doesn't matter. Just place a marker at the halfway point of the cast-on stitches to denote the beginning of the round. If you know how long you want your sleeves to be, you can make a calculation to add shaping. You can either shape the sleeve simply so it tapers to fit your wrist, or, if you want, you can decrease down to the elbow and then work spaced increases down to the cuff for a bell shaped-sleeve.

Unisex Drop- (or Modified Drop-) Sleeve Pullover Formula

The drop-sleeve sweater, or drop-shoulder sweater, is one of the simplest of all sweaters to knit top-down. This traditionally-shaped garment has practically no shaping at all, so it lends itself nicely to colorwork, color bands, and slip-stitch motifs. Think of a drop-sleeve sweater as a simple rectangle that is knit from the shoulders down with little or no shaping except for a hole for the neck opening, and then joined in the round at the underarms and worked seamlessly to the hem.

The difference between a true drop-sleeve sweater and a modified one is its width at the shoulders. The drop-sleeve version is simply one half of the total body circumference at its initial cast on, or at the top of the shoulders, so the body of the sweater will drape over the shoulders, even as far as the halfway point between the edge of the shoulder and the elbow. A modified drop-sleeve sweater is a little narrower, so the initial cast-on would be several inches narrower, and later, when it is time to join the body in the round, stitches are cast on at the underarms to accommodate the desired circumference; the garment is worked in rounds down to the hem. Looking at the two, the only real difference is that the modified drop-sleeve sweater's shoulder lines don't drop as far as the regular dropped sleeve does; in fact, in some patterns, the shoulder lines don't drop at all, but fit the shoulders. Take a look at the Wasabi pattern on page 128 for an example of a drop shoulder. Although it has a construction that is a little different than the "recipe" I'll give you here, you could easily follow its steps to make a similar design.

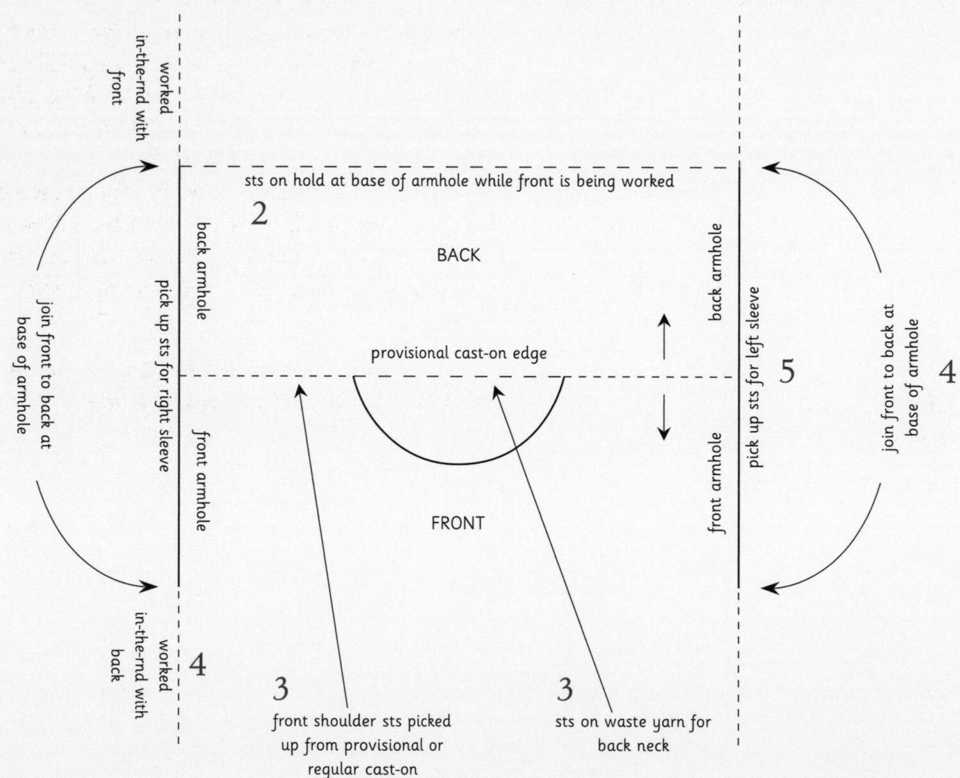

1 Make a swatch and decide what you want the body circumference to be, including extra inches for ease, if desired.

(Body circumference ÷ 2) x stitch gauge = number of stitches to cast on for the back (you can do these provisionally or, if you don't mind a little seam at the shoulders, do a regular cast-on).

2 Knit down to between 1″ and 2″ beyond the wearer's underarm. Place the back stitches on waste yarn.

3 Decide how you want to divide the front stitches for your neck opening. You can either split the total number of back stitches into thirds and place each outer third stitches onto the needle (or pick up that number if you did a regular cast-on), or measure the desired breadth of the neck opening and subtract that number of stitches from the back stitches and place one-half of the remainder onto your needle for each shoulder. Place the neck stitches on waste yarn.

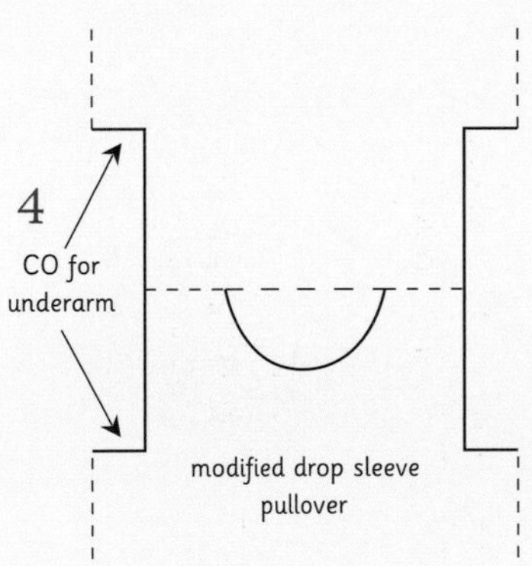

4 For a straight neck opening (like a boatneck, for example), work the first set of shoulder stitches, cast on the number of neck stitches required, then continue across the next set of shoulder stitches. Continue working flat the same number of rows as the back, join, and work in rounds down to the hem. (Of course, if you are working a modified version of the drop-sleeve sweater, add the required number of stitches under each underarm to increase the body circumference to the desired number of inches.) For a high neck that will appear like a crew neck once the neck edging is added, work the two shoulders separately without any shaping until they have come to the level of the collarbone, and then cast on the required number of center neck stitches, join the fronts, and work the same number of rows as you did for the back, before joining in the round and working toward the hem.

5 Once the body is complete, you can focus on the sleeves. Pick up sleeve stitches around the armhole and count stitches. Using your gauge as your guide, take your stitch count and divide it by the number of stitches per inch. This will be the resulting upper arm circumference. If you are fine with that circumference (consider, too, that drop shoulders usually have several inches of positive ease), work on down toward the cuff and add spaced decreases so that the sleeve will fit your wrist. When working these sleeves, it's important to try on as you go because the sleeves measure much shorter with this type of sweater.

6 If desired, pick up stitches around the neck opening and finish it off any way you like.

SPECIAL TECHNIQUES

Backward Loop CO: When working the CO at the end of a row, *wind yarn around thumb clockwise, insert right-hand needle into the front of the loop on the thumb, remove thumb and tighten st on needle; repeat from * for remaining sts needed. When working the CO at the beginning of a row, work as above, inserting left-hand needle instead of right-hand needle into the loop on the thumb.

Kitchener Stitch: Using a blunt yarn needle, thread a length of yarn approximately 4 times the length of the section to be joined. Hold the pieces to be joined wrong sides together, with the needles holding the sts parallel, both ends pointing to the right. Working from right to left, insert the yarn needle into the first st on the front needle as if to purl, pull yarn through, leaving the st on the needle; insert the yarn needle into the first st on the back needle as if to knit, pull the yarn through, leaving the st on the needle; *insert the yarn needle into the first st on the front needle as if to knit, pull the yarn through, remove the st from the needle; insert the yarn needle into the next st on the front needle as if to purl, pull the yarn through, leave the st on the needle; insert the yarn needle into the first st on the back needle as if to purl, pull the yarn through, remove the st from the needle; insert the yarn needle into the next st on the back needle as if to knit, pull the yarn through, leave the st on the needle. Repeat from *, working 3 or 4 sts at a time, then go back and adjust the tension to match the pieces being joined. When 1 st remains on each needle, cut the yarn and pass through the last 2 sts to fasten off.

Long-Tail CO: Leaving a tail with about 1" of yarn for each st to be CO, make a slipknot in the yarn and place it on the right-hand needle, with the tail end to the front and the working end to the back. Insert the thumb and forefinger of your left hand between the strands of yarn so that the working end is around your forefinger and the tail end is around your thumb "slingshot" fashion; * insert the tip of the right-hand needle into the front loop on the thumb, hook the strand of yarn coming from the forefinger from back to front, and draw it through the loop on your thumb; remove your thumb from the loop and pull on the working yarn to tighten the new st on the right-hand needle; return your thumb and forefinger to their original positions, and repeat from * for remaining sts needed.

Placing Stitches on Waste Yarn: Many patterns in this book instruct you to place live stitches on waste yarn, which will not distort the stitches like a holder will. Simply thread waste yarn in a contrasting color onto a tapestry needle. Then, using the threaded tapestry needle, slip each stitch from the needle onto the tapestry needle and thread the waste yarn through live stitches. Pull an extra several inches through the stitches to be held, and cut the waste yarn.

Reading Charts: Unless otherwise specified in the instructions, when working straight, read charts from right to left for RS rows and from left to right for WS rows. Row numbers are written at the beginning of each row. Numbers on the right indicate RS rows; numbers on the left indicate WS rows. When working circularly, read all rounds from right to left.

Reverse Stockinette Stitch (Rev St st): Purl on RS rows, knit on WS rows when working straight; purl every round when working circularly.

Stockinette Stitch (St st): Knit on RS rows, purl on WS rows when working straight; knit every round when working circularly.

Stranded (Fair Isle) Colorwork Method: When more than one color is used per row, carry color(s) not in use loosely across the WS of the work. Be sure to secure all colors at the beginning and end of the rows to prevent holes.

Three-Needle BO: Place the sts to be joined onto 2 same-size needles; hold the pieces to be joined with the RSs facing each other and the needles parallel, both pointing to the right. Holding both needles in your left hand, using working yarn and a third needle the same size or one size larger, insert the third needle into the first st on the front needle, then into the first st on the back needle; knit these 2 sts together; *knit the next st from each needle together (2 sts on the right-hand needle); pass the first st over the second st to BO one st. Repeat from * until 1 st remains on the third needle; cut yarn and fasten off.

Yarnover (yo) Other than Beginning of Row: Bring the yarn forward (to the purl position), then place it in position to work the next st. If the next st is to be knit, bring the yarn over the needle and knit; if the next st is to be purled, bring the yarn over the needle and then forward again to the purl position and purl. Work the yo in pattern on the next row unless instructed otherwise.

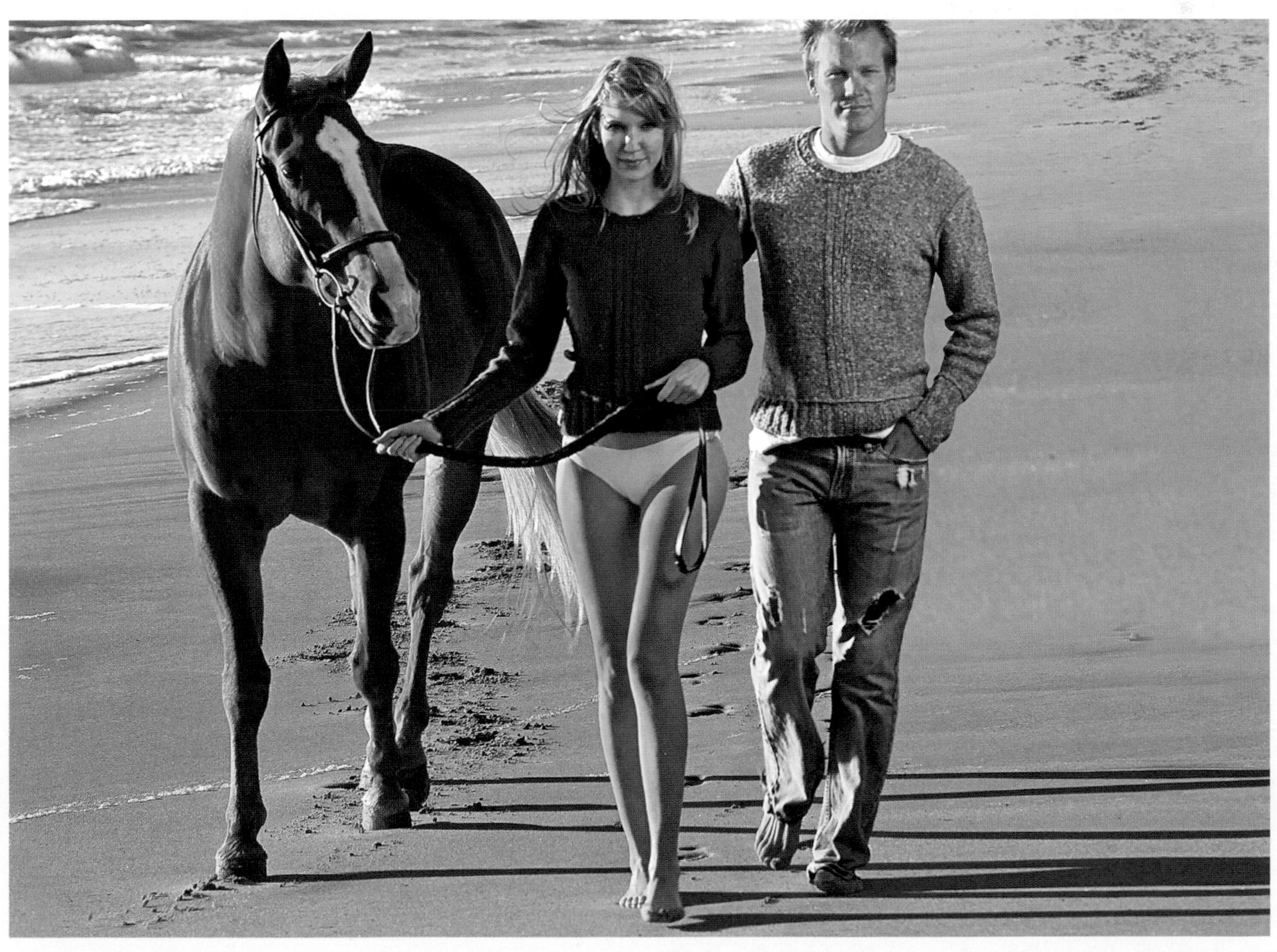

Provisional Cast-On Techniques

A provisional cast-on is used whenever you want to create a starting point in your knitting from which you can work later in the opposite direction. When you cast on provisionally, there are no seams, so I like to cast on provisionally at the top of the shoulder when working top down. This makes the tops of my shoulders look nice and smooth. *Note: For larger sizes, or when using extra heavy-weight yarn, you may find it preferable to go ahead and use a conventional cast-on and pick up and knit the shoulder stitches, working your way down the front as in the pattern. This will create a seam much like a sewn-in one without disrupting the integrity of the pattern. If you like, you can hand-sew a length of binding tape at the shoulders for further reinforcement.* This technique is also helpful at the bottom of a garment to add length later. Using a provisional cast-on also comes in handy when you're not quite sure if you have enough yarn to complete a project. In the case of socks, if you use a provisional cast-on, you can work both of the feet first (from the top up), then separate your leftover yarn into two equal balls and finish the cuffs knowing you won't run out.

There are several ways to cast on provisionally. My favorite method is the Long-Tail Cast-On version.

LONG-TAIL PROVISIONAL CAST-ON

1 Find some slippery yarn from an odd ball in your stash that is approximately the same gauge as your working yarn (that is, the yarn you are using for your project). We can call this "waste yarn." Make sure it is in a contrasting color.

2 Make a slipknot with both your working yarn and your waste yarn held together and place the slipknot onto your needle.

3 Set up for your Long-Tail Cast-On, but put the waste yarn over your thumb and the working yarn over your index finger.

4 Cast on as usual, but notice as you do this that the waste yarn makes a nice chain at the bottom of your needle. If you make a working loop (one that sits on your needle) with your waste yarn, then you've made a mistake. Cast on the number of stitches required in the pattern, but don't count the original slipknot as a stitch.

5 When you are done with your cast on, before you cut the waste yarn, check to see that all the working yarn is looped on the needle and the waste yarn is "chained" below it.

6 Cut your waste yarn, turn your work, and begin working your stitches as called for in the pattern. When you reach the slipknot, drop it. Let it hang while you knit.

GETTING YOUR STITCHES BACK ON THE NEEDLES

1 Recall that you made a slipknot with your waste yarn and working yarn and cast on stitches from there. Place your knitting on a table with the right side facing and with the slipknot on your right.

2 Carefully untie the slipknot and begin to unravel the stitches. As you do this, you will see a loop of working yarn. That is your first stitch. Pluck out the waste yarn and place the loop of working yarn on your needle.

3 Continue across all the stitches, plucking out the waste yarn as you go. I use the other side of my circular needle or a spare needle to do so. Keep a pair of scissors nearby in case the yarn sticks so you can carefully cut the waste yarn as you move across the row.

CROCHET HOOK PROVISIONAL CAST-ON

If you are relatively comfortable using a crochet hook and have one the same size as your working needles, there are two methods of creating a provisional cast-on using waste yarn and a crochet hook. With the first method, you will cast onto your knitting needle directly, using a crochet hook.

1 Begin with waste yarn in a similar weight, preferably a slippery yarn in a contrast color that is easy to see. Make a slipknot and place it on the crochet hook. Hold the crochet hook in your right hand, above the knitting needle in your left hand. Take the working yarn under the knitting needle and yarn over the crochet hook.

2 Crochet a chain stitch by pulling the yarn held on the crochet hook through the loop on the end of the hook. Take the working yarn back under the knitting needle and yarnover the crochet hook. Repeat this movement until the correct number of stitches has been cast onto the knitting needle.

3 Cut the yarn and fasten off. Work knitting stitches directly into cast-on stitches.

HOW TO REMOVE THE CROCHET HOOK PROVISIONAL CAST-ON

1 Beginning with the fastened-off end of the crocheted cast on, unravel the tail end from the last loop.

2 Pull on it carefully to expose a live stitch. Place the live stitch on a knitting needle. Continue across the row until all your stitches are on the needle.

CROCHET CHAIN PROVISIONAL CAST-ON

1 Begin with waste yarn in a similar weight, preferably a slippery yarn in a contrast color that is easy to see. Make a slipknot and place it on the crochet hook. Crochet a chain that is several chain stitches longer than the number of stitches required. Fasten off the last stitch and cut the yarn.

2 Tie a knot in the tail of yarn to serve as a reminder as to which end will "unzip."

3 Looking at the chain, note that one side is smooth and the other side has bumps. Using your knitting needle, knit a stitch directly into the bump "loops." Continue across, being careful to knit only into the bumps, until you have cast on the required number of stitches.

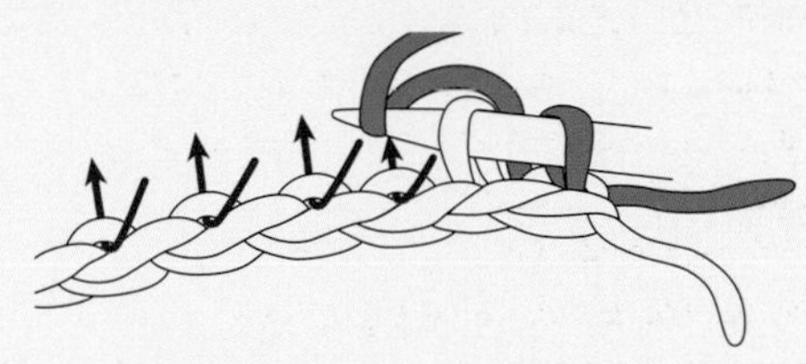

HOW TO REMOVE THE CROCHET HOOK PROVISIONAL CAST-ON

1 Look for the knot tied into one end of the crocheted chain. Untie the knot.

2 Carefully pull on waste yarn to "unzip" one stitch to expose a live knit loop. Place knit loop onto knitting needle. Continue across the row until all your stitches are on the needle.

Short-Row Shaping

Short rows are partial rows of knitting that curve or shape knitted pieces. The result is that one section has more rows than the other, but the relative length of the piece isn't affected. In this book I use short rows to shape all sorts of things: sleeve caps, shoulder slopes on the tops of sweaters, or to shape the neckline of the front of a sweater so it swoops in toward the center, creating a drapelike effect without affecting the garment's overall length. Ladies in need of bust shaping will often use short row shaping to create a "pocket" in the front of the garment so their sweaters don't rise up in the front (see page 18). After all the short rows have been completed, work one final row across all the stitches, hiding the wraps as you encounter them, and continue working either flat or in-the-round, according to the pattern.

To make short rows undetectable, you will want to make a smooth transition between the edge where one row is worked and the edge that has the extra row. You do this by wrapping a slipped stitch, which prevents a hole from forming when you turn and work across the other side of the piece. Knit stitches and purl stitches are treated differently:

WRAPPING KNIT STITCHES

1 Work across the piece to the place where you want to end your short row. With the yarn in back, slip the next stitch purlwise.

2 Bring the yarn between the needles to the front of the work.

3 Slip the slipped stitch back to the left-hand needle. Turn the work and bring the yarn to the working side between the needles. One stitch is now wrapped.

4 When you have finished your short rows, you need to hide the wraps. To do this with a knit stitch, work to the wrapped stitch. Insert the right-hand needle under the wrap, knitwise, then into the wrapped stitch. Knit the 2 stitches together.

WRAPPING PURL STITCHES

1 Work across the piece to the place where you want to end your short row. With the yarn in front, slip the next stitch purlwise.

2 Bring the yarn between the needles to the back of the work.

3 Slip the slipped stitch back to the left-hand needle. Turn the work and bring the yarn to the working side between the needles. One stitch is now wrapped.

4 When you have finished your short rows, you need to hide the wraps. To do this on a purled stitch, work to the wrapped stitch. Insert the right-hand needle from behind into the back loop of the wrap and place it on the left-hand needle. Purl it together with the stitch on the left-hand needle.

ABBREVIATIONS

BO: Bind off

Ch: Chain

Circ: Circular

Cn: Cable needle

CO: Cast on

Dpn: Double-pointed needle(s)

K: Knit

K1-f/b: Knit into front loop and back loop of same stitch to increase 1 stitch.

K1-f/b/f: Knit into the front loop, back loop, then front loop of the same stitch to increase 2 stitches.

K1-tbl: Knit 1 stitch through the back loop, twisting the stitch.

K2tog: Knit 2 stitches together.

K3tog: Knit 3 stitches together.

M1 or m1-l (make 1-left slanting): With the tip of the left-hand needle inserted from front to back, lift the strand between the 2 needles onto the left-hand needle; knit the strand through the back loop to increase 1 stitch.

P: Purl

P1-f/b: Purl into front loop and back loop of same stitch to increase 1 stitch.

P1-f/b/f: Purl into the front loop, back loop, then front loop of the same stitch to increase 2 stitches.

P2tog: Purl 2 stitches together.

P3tog: Purl 3 stitches together.

Pm: Place marker

Psso (pass slipped stitch over): Pass slipped stitch on right-hand needle over the stitches indicated in the instructions, as in binding off.

Rnd(s): Round(s)

RS: Right side

Sc (single crochet): Insert hook into next stitch and draw up a loop (2 loops on hook), yarn over and draw through both loops on hook.

Sk2p (double decrease): Slip the next stitch knitwise to the right-hand needle, k2tog, pass the slipped stitch over the stitch from the k2tog.

Skp (slip, knit, pass): Slip the next stitch knitwise to the right-hand needle, knit, pass the slipped stitch over the knit stitch.

Sl st (crochet slip stitch): Insert the hook in a stitch, yarn over the hook, and draw through the loop on the hook.

Sm: Slip marker

Ssk (slip, slip, knit): Slip the next 2 stitches to the right-hand needle one at a time as if to knit; return them back to the left-hand needle one at a time in their new orientation; knit them together through the back loop(s).

Sssk: Same as ssk, but worked on next 3 stitches.

St(s): Stitch(es)

Tbl: Through the back loop

Tog: Together

WS: Wrong side

Wrp-t: Wrap and turn (see Short-Row Shaping, opposite)

Wyib: With yarn in back

Wyif: With yarn in front

Yo: Yarnover (see Special Techniques, page 153)

YARN SOURCES

BERROCO, INC.
P.O. Box 367
14 Elmdale Road
Uxbridge, MA 01569
(508) 278-2527
www.berroco.com

BLUE HERON YARNS
29532 Canvasback Drive, Suite 8
Easton, MD 21601
(410) 819-0401
www.blueheronyarns.com

BLUE SKY ALPACAS, INC.
P.O. Box 88
Cedar, MN 55011
(888) 460-8862
www.blueskyalpacas.com

BROWN SHEEP COMPANY, INC.
100662 County Road 16
Mitchell, NE 69357
(800) 826-9136
www.brownsheep.com

CASCADE YARNS
P.O. Box 58168
Tukwila, WA 98138
(800) 548-1048
www.cascadeyarns.com

ELSEBETH LAVOLD YARNS
Distributor: Knitting Fever, Inc.

GGH YARNS
Distributor: Muench Yarns, Inc.

KNIT ONE, CROCHET TOO, INC.
91 Tandberg Trail, Unit 6
Windham, ME 04062
(207) 892-9625
www.knitonecrochettoo.com

KNITTING FEVER, INC.
P.O. Box 336
315 Bayview Avenue
Amityville, NY 11701
(516) 546-3600
www.knittingfever.com

KOIGU WOOL DESIGNS
P.O. Box 158
Chatsworth, Ontario NOH IGO
Canada
(888) 765-WOOL
www.koigu.com

LANA GROSSA YARNS
Distributor: Muench Yarns, Inc.

LORNA'S LACES
4229 North Honore Street
Chicago, IL 60613
(773) 935-3803
www.lornaslaces.net

MALABRIGO YARN
Wholesale Info:
(786) 866-8167

MIRASOL YARNS
Distributor: Knitting Fever, Inc.

MUENCH YARNS, INC.
1323 Scott Street
Petaluma, CA 94954
(800) 733-9276
www.muenchyarns.com

NASHUA HANDKNITS
Distributor: Westminster Fibers

ROWAN/RYC YARNS
Distributor: Westminster Fibers

SHIBUIKNITS, LLC
1101 SW Alder Street
Portland, OR 97205
(503) 595-5898
www.shibuiknits.com

SPUD & CHLOE
(see Blue Sky Alpacas, Inc.)
www.spudandchloe.com

SUSAN BATES
Distributed by Coats and Clark
P.O. Box 12229
Greenville, SC 29612

O-WOOL
(Tunney Wool Company)
915 N 28th Street
Philadelphia, PA 19130
(888) 673-0260
www.o-wool.com

PAGEWOOD FARM
San Pedro, CA
(310) 403-7880
www.pagewoodfarm.com

REYNOLD'S YARNS
Division of JCA, Inc.
35 Scales Lane
Townsend, MA 01469
(978) 597-8794
www.jcacrafts.com

SIRDAR
Distributor: Knitting Fever, Inc.

STITCH DIVA
www.stitchdiva.com

TAHKI/STACY CHARLES, INC.
70-30 80th Street, Building 36
Ridgewood, NY 11385
(800) 338-YARN
www.tahkistacycharles.com

WESTMINSTER FIBERS
165 Ledge Street
Nashua, NH 03060
(800) 445-9276
www.westminsterfibers.com

ACKNOWLEDGMENTS

The hardest part about writing a book—especially a knitting book—is the time that you spend away from your loved ones. I am especially thankful that my husband, Theron, and my daughter, Mia, have been extraordinarily understanding and patient when I've been holed up in my office or when they've had to maneuver around the piles of yarn and unfinished projects lying around the house. They are both experts in picking up projects and gingerly moving them without disturbing a stitch!

My sincere thanks go to Melanie Falick for taking me on in the first place, and to Liana Allday, my editor and someone who I view as my most likely partner in crime. (If only we lived closer!) Liana's thoughtful editing makes me sound more like me. Not only that, Liana and Melanie's skill in organizing and reorganizing the material is mind-boggling. It amazes me to look through these pages. I keep pinching myself, wondering, "Did I really do this?" I've come to realize that this is truly a team effort. Without Melanie and Liana, it just wouldn't be the book that you are holding in your hands. Anna Christian is a part of this team, too—she's the graphic designer on the Custom Knits series, and her talent has turned both books into truly cohesive bodies of work.

I am grateful for Sue McCain, my technical editor, who also worked on *Custom Knits*. She's smart as smart can be and practically reads my mind. Thanks also to Robin Melanson, who lent her second pair of eyes to the patterns and technical bits, and to Ana Deboo, who did the proofreading.

Although I normally knit each of the samples in my books, from time to time I need a little help. Erica Hernandez and Leah Coccari-Swift expertly knit a few garments for *Custom Knits 2*. Thank you! I also want to say thanks to my friend Allison Migliaccio, who has been a constant source of support. When I've panicked about a deadline or a pattern—or just from the sheer pressure of writing a book—she has talked me down, given me a ride somewhere, or told me something funny to take my mind to a better place.

Finally, when the manuscript and patterns for this book were complete, it was time to choose a stylist and a photographer. With the success of *Custom Knits*, it made total sense to bring in the same team: Mark Auria and Printer Hall. Mark styled the looks in this book, and his eye for color and finding ways to show off my sweaters are talents that cannot be duplicated (not to mention his great enthusiasm). Mark has become a close and beloved friend; thanks to Caroline Greeven, my agent, who introduced us. The photographer, Printer Hall, has a similar enthusiasm, and really knows how to find the perfect light and bring the models to life; he's also a hoot to work with. Red Dodge did all the makeup and hair. She's a similar "hoot," and her work is divine.

Last but not least, thank you to the knitters. Without you, my life would be half as much fun.

WENDY BERNARD is a knitwear designer based in Southern California. She is the author of *Custom Knits* and the creator of the popular blog Knit and Tonic (KnitandTonic.net). Her knitwear patterns have been published online by Knitty and Stitch Diva Studios, in the magazines *Interweave Knits*, *Knitscene*, and *Yarn Forward*, in the books *No Sheep for You* and *Brave New Knits*, and in a DVD series teaching top-down knitting techniques. Her wholesale pattern line is available through Deep South Fibers.

PRINTER HALL is a Southern California–based photographer with 25 years of experience working on editorial and advertising projects. Among his clients are Four Seasons Hotels, American Express, and Bank of America.

MARK AURIA is a Los Angeles–based art director and wardrobe stylist who has worked in advertising, print, and television. His most recent clients include American and European fashion magazines and the corporations Zink, Pepsi, LG, and Apple.

ADDITIONAL CREDITS:
Camera Assistants: Theron Tan and Robert Larson
Makeup: Red Dodge
Assistant Photo Stylist: Darius Bossinas
Wardrobe Assistant: Jessica Yoon
Food Styling: Janet Rorschach of zhianriverreed.wordpress.com
Horse Trainer: Peggy Lane
Modeling Agency: Brand Model and Talent
Talent: Angel Archer, Bruce Brenon, Bianca and Chiara D'Ambrosio, Anna Easteden, Alan Jouban, Carolyn Stotes, Mia Tan, Max Volkan
Contributing Clothing: Cordelialifestyle.com, Sheepiedoodles.com, Shopelectrify.com